The Invisible Customer

Customer Quality Management:
how to identify and develop
potential through building
relationships– and make your
enterprise take off!

Cobus van Graan
Dr Chris Crozier

Note for Librarians: A cataloguing record for this book is available from Library and Archives Canada at www.collectionscanada.ca/amicus/index-e.html
ISBN 1-4251-2250-7

Printed in Victoria, BC, Canada. Printed on paper with minimum 30% recycled fibre.
Trafford's print shop runs on "green energy" from solar, wind and other environmentally-friendly power sources.

Offices in Canada, USA, Ireland and UK

Book sales for North America and international:
Trafford Publishing, 6E–2333 Government St.,
Victoria, BC V8T 4P4 CANADA
phone 250 383 6864 (toll-free 1 888 232 4444)
fax 250 383 6804; email to orders@trafford.com
Book sales in Europe:
Trafford Publishing (UK) Limited, 9 Park End Street, 2nd Floor
Oxford, UK OX1 1HH UNITED KINGDOM
phone +44 (0)1865 722 113 (local rate 0845 230 9601)
facsimile +44 (0)1865 722 868; info.uk@trafford.com
Order online at:
trafford.com/07-0651

10 9 8 7 6 5 4 3 2

Foreword

Customer Quality Management (CQM) will change forever the way you see your customers, and how you treat them. It's not rocket science, but the results can be explosive growth of your business.

The term Customer Quality Management was coined by the authors in the course of looking for a concise term that would encapsulate the principles that had proven so effective in re-energising businesses. It turns the emphasis from mechanistic counting of customers and sales calls to examining the *quality* of the customers and the *quality* of contacts with the customers.

In writing this book, our aim has been to keep it practical and informative, rather than being too theoretical a guide to the principles and practice of CQM.

There are many examples and case studies throughout the text to illustrate the principles of CQM. However, the company names used are fictitious, and in some cases the industry area is also changed. Companies – our clients – who have successfully applied CQM are often jealous of their "secret formula": where competitors are wondering what hit them, our clients want to keep it that way.

Indeed, some clients have the authors on retainer **not** to approach their competitors.

Nonetheless, all case studies, the figures cited for profit, turnover or market share growth, and the timescales involved, are drawn from life.

The Invisible Customer

Acknowledgements

Creating a book always involves more people than just the author or authors, both in the creation of the book itself and in the process of acquiring the experience and knowledge that are distilled and embodied in the book.

I would like to acknowledge and thank the people who played a significant part in variously teaching, guiding, inspiring or encouraging me in both my personal life and the development of my own business and sales expertise:

The late Jamie McGregor: A National Sales Manager from Abbott Laboratories

Wayne Brunyee: Sales and Marketing Director from Eli Lilly

Bill Gibson: Chairman of Knowledge Brokers International

Simon Nash: Sales Director of Fintec

Dr Chris Crozier: Business owner and co-author

Cobus van Graan

My thanks go to my wife Jenny for her support during the writing of this book, and for coming up with a title that so aptly captured its spirit.

Chris Crozier

Our joint thanks go to Simon Nash, Cecile Wiltshire and Wouter Snyman for their reviews and constructive comments on the book, and to Graham van der Westhuizen for the delightful dragon he created to highlight the Sales Myths.

The Authors

The Invisible Customer

Contents

1   THE INVISIBLE CUSTOMER..1

   Introduction 1

      Why businesses are stalling................................5

      Enter Customer Quality Management..................7

   Chapter Summary – The Invisible Customer...................11

2   CUSTOMER QUALITY MANAGEMENT..................13

      Call Quality Management.................................17

      CRM Software 18

   Chapter Summary – Customer Quality Management....................20

3   THE THREE PILLARS OF BUSINESS STRATEGY........................21

   Company Alignment..21

      Customerculture 23

   Business Objectives..26

      Defining Quality of Business............................27

      Types of Objectives 28

   Market Opportunity..28

   Business Resources..30

   Alignment 31

      Achieving Alignment 33

   Chapter Summary – The Three Pillars of Business Strategy.........40

4   PREPARING FOR CUSTOMER QUALITY MANAGEMENT.....41

      Defining Quality 42

      What makes a quality customer?....................42

   Focus Factors...43

      Too much or not enough Gold.........................51

      Identifying focus market segments 51

      The Second Dimension.....................................54

      Separate the Urgent from the Important 59

      Multi-Level Selling...61

      Identifying the Business Influencers 62

Understanding Business Influencers...63

Chapter Summary – Preparing for Customer Quality Management

....**66**

5   BUILDING RELATIONSHIPS IN A CQM ENVIRONMENT.......67

Sales Conversion Rate: Frequent Contact Works 67

The Numbers Game 67

Proactive Targeting...70

Activity Consistency 70

Smoothing out the roller-coaster 73

Chapter Summary – Building Relationships in a CQM

Environment 76

6   COMBINING FREQUENCY AND VALUE-ADD.....................77

Add Value!..79

The Yin and Yang of Sales 79

Be interesting, be different..82

Getting the Mix Right..83

Business Influencers – Matching Strategies to People 83

Chapter Summary – Combining Frequency and Value-Add 90

7   KNOW YOUR CUSTOMER..91

The submarine commander's dilemma 91

Getting away from WIIFM 91

Gathering Information 93

Practical examples 94

Chapter Summary – Know Your Customer 98

8   PUTTING IT INTO PRACTICE...99

The Four Pillar Business Plan 101

First Steps..108

Explain the Strategy and Vision..108

Develop Focus Factors and Contact Frequency Plans.................110

Measurement and Reporting...111

Structured Coaching from First-Line Managers 112

Making It Happen 114
   A Typical Timeline...116
Resistance to CQM 118
Chapter Summary – Putting it into Practice 122

9   BRINGING IT ALL TOGETHER................................123
   Strategic Skills Development...123
   Sales and Management Roles 124
   Alignment and company resources...............................124
   Buy-in 124
Getting Buy-In...125
   Buy-in Levels 125
   Consistency Is Key 127
   Driving culture change..127
Chapter Summary – Bringing It All Together................130

10   KEEPING IT ALIVE 131
Incentive Schemes 131
Creative Targeting 134
Sales Support Personnel...136
Training 137
Chapter Summary – Keeping It Alive.............................138

11   IN CONCLUSION...139

INDEX...143

The Myths of Sales

 Myth 1: All customers are good customers (p. 8)

 Myth 2: Last year's sales indicate this year's top customers (p. 14)

 Myth 3: High call rates lead to high sales (p. 17)

 Myth 4: All Departments / Divisions work towards a common goal (p. 22)

 Myth 5: Support departments will give top customers top service (p. 30)

 Myth 6: Last year's top customers should be this year's top customers (p. 42)

 Myth 7: Sales people target customers who are best for the company (p. 52)

 Myth 8: Busy salespeople are an indicator of sales (p. 60)

 Myth 9: Selling is about talking business (p. 74)

 Myth 10: Sales people use all the available resources and tools to make contact with customers (p. 78)

 Myth 11: First-line managers understand that their role is to coach and develop their sales people (p. 112)

 Myth 12: Top salespeople know what they do right (p. 113)

The Invisible Customer

1

The Invisible Customer

Introduction

We are all surrounded by invisible people. You walk past them all the time, on the street, in shopping malls, in the corridors of businesses. It's not that they are not able to be seen, it's that you simply don't see them. They melt into the background because they don't get past the filters that your mind has put in place.

We are the same in business: we are surrounded by customers that we don't see. Our filters are set to let the wrong customers come to our attention: usually the ones that we have been doing business with already and who are amongst our current top customers. Even with these customers, we see only a portion: there might be a much greater part hiding, iceberg-like, out of our sight, buried under the water level.

The problem is that traditionally companies don't focus on the right criteria when evaluating prospective or existing customers. If you want to grow your business you must look at your customers and prospects through the lens of *potential*. How big *could* this customer be? One of the novel aspects of this approach is that you start evaluating both customers and prospects using a common yardstick, which is their *potential* value to your business. How to deal with them in the light of the ratio of potential to actual business is a secondary consideration.

The results can be startling: identifying your top potential customers and cultivating them appropriately on the one hand, and on the other hand stopping spending scarce sales and support resources on customers and prospects who do not have high potential, will transform your business faster and more dramatically than the tired old mantras of work harder and improve your sales skills.

Some of this book is old news. The starting points are the 80/20 principle, and that business is about relationships. The 80/20 principle is well known in business: 80% of your profits come from 20% of your customers; 80% of your business comes from 20% of your sales team. And it's hardly news that business is about relationships.

What *is* new in this book is how to apply those principles in practice, how to make them work for you to increase your sales dramatically. We present a methodology based on the concept of managing the *quality* of your customers and your interactions with your customers, whereas conventional customer relationship management tends to focus on *quantity*.

Business is about people doing business with people, and the sharp end of business is about people trying to sell to people. There are metres of books on bookstore shelves about sales training and sales strategy, and a whole sub-industry of motivational speakers who, for a substantial fee, will deliver an inspiring pep-talk that will leave everyone feeling warm and (temporarily) energised. Small fortunes are spent on consultants and trainers. And yet, after all the money spent on books and presentations and training courses, businesses are still failing to find the spark that will set their sales soaring.

One reason for the lack of results is that amidst the wealth of training material there is a conspicuous dearth of material aimed at the National Sales Manager or Sales Director, and even less that gets to the heart of building sales by building relationships. Relationships are the foundation of any business, but your typical sales manual talks about call rates and frequency, brings in the 80/20 principle without either placing it in the proper context or showing how to implement it on a national or global level, and fails to address the interdependency of sales strategy, business resources, market opportunity and business objectives.

This book has been written because we believe a great deal of money is being wasted on inappropriate tools and ineffective training, leading to an even greater sum of missed profits. One of the biggest culprits in leading businesses astray is technology: as the world gets more complex, many attempt to fight fire with fire but end up even further from the basic wisdom that good business is about people and relationships, and introduce excessive, or more often, inappropriate automation at grave risk to the business.

No book about business today can escape reference to the effects of technology. Technology, and particularly Information Technology, is transforming the business world at a furious pace. This much is common knowledge, but the side effects of the rate of change are not always so obvious. Rapid change is exciting and opens up fresh possibilities, but human nature has not changed fundamentally in the last decade or two, nor even in the last century or two, and part of our nature is that we need time to absorb change, to internalise it and build up a basis of intuition and instinct that we call common sense. When conditions change faster than our ability to become comfortable with the changes, common sense flies out of the window.

Whilst we must necessarily refer to the tools and effects of technology, our theme is primarily about people skills, strategy and understanding how to grow your business through understanding how your customers fit your business strategy and available resources. Technology can be as much a hindrance as a help in this.

Young bloods with fantastic visions trumpet new vistas and declare old paradigms dead. Older heads, no longer so confident of their wisdom as the ground rules appear to be shifting under their feet, are often cowed by the vociferous vanguard of this year's New Era prophets. Some, like Warren Buffet, held their ground: when the world was falling over itself to invest in the dot com start-ups Buffet held back, saying he did not invest in companies he did not understand. If the rest of the world had followed his advice, vast fortunes would not have been lost in the subsequent crashes. (And vast fortunes would not have been made by those who promoted the "New Economy" businesses then cashed out at the right time.)

At the root of the unease many managers feel, and indeed the reason so many businesses are wasting huge amounts of resources in failed technology investments, is the fact that the great majority of business people no longer understand the fundamentals of one of their biggest costs: information technology. Arthur C Clarke once stated that "Any sufficiently advanced technology is indistinguishable from magic", and bluntly, to most business people, their companies are run on an infrastructure of magic.

The trouble with magic is that you don't understand what it can and can't do for you, and you can't properly assess the claims of the self-professed wizards who are selling you their spells and potions to cure the ills you perceive in your business. The analogy goes further: like charlatan purveyors of snake oil cures, they have all the excuses for non-delivery of results. If it didn't work, it's because you didn't follow instructions properly. Your warts didn't vanish? Did you apply the ointment at midnight with a new moon? Your data warehousing project that cost you millions to implement failed to produce any tangible bottom-line results? Did you train your staff properly and gather the right data and analyse it correctly and …

The dot com crash taught a lot of people that business is business. The environment you operate in might be changing, rules may be shifting, but fundamentals do not change all that quickly. Customers are still people, and people still like to deal with people.

How can people believe the current crop of vendors offering the latest "ultimate solution" when history has proven nearly all the previous messiahs wrong? The gurus who told us the mainframe was dead and decentralised client/server computing was the new way forward have been supplanted by the gurus telling us that centralised computing on demand is the new answer. The lemming-like rush to outsource everything possible is slowing and turning into a trend to pull functions back under the business' direct control. And so it goes on, yet we continue to put faith in the magicians telling us that the next spell *will* work.

Technology allows us to track and measure activities to a degree undreamt of a decade or two ago, we can accumulate vast amounts of data about our customers, their buying habits, and our sales people. We can automate processes in the name of efficiency and communicate with, and manage our relationship with, our customers using the latest Customer Relationship Management (CRM) software and extract statistics and reports in volumes beyond any hope of usefulness. None of this is of any use if we are not doing the right things.

Waving a technological wand at the challenges of building business is all too often an exercise in doing the wrong things faster and more efficiently than ever before. It's time to re-focus on the fundamentals, and in business the fundamentals are people, strategy and resources.

Why businesses are stalling

Businesses get stuck in the doldrums for various reasons, almost always in combination. Some factors are not controllable, for example: regulatory changes, economic downturns, exchange rates. Some are controllable but very hard to change, such as senior management composition or lack of direction from the Board. Others are very much controllable if the management will is there, and these are:

- The types of customers you have.

- The focus of your sales team.

- Lack of performance metrics: e.g. pipeline management.

- Incorrect performance metrics: e.g. call rates tell you very little about the effectiveness of your sales team.

- Skills shortages: e.g. strategic skills, sales skills.

- Organisational design: e.g. inappropriate or unclear reporting structures and definitions of responsibilities.

The first two points are about determining who controls your business: you, or your customers? If you are reactively responding to the massed voices of your customer base without understanding where your profitability comes from and, more important, where your best opportunities for growing profitability (or market share, or turnover – whatever your primary goal is) lie, then your customers are controlling your business. Applying the principles of Customer Quality Management (CQM) leads to **you** taking control of your business.

Performance metrics are the indicators that tell you how you are doing. A successful sales strategy cannot be built in isolation. You have to be able to tell if you are being successful, which may sound silly but more than one company has gone into liquidation whilst sales appeared to be booming because the sales success was not being measured properly. If you need to generate cash from operations but you are generating lots of business that is absorbing cash flow, you are in trouble. Hence, the performance metrics must be right.

To achieve your goals and metrics you have to have the skills in place, and this means training and implementation follow-up to grow the skills needed.

To determine the right metrics and skills requirements you must be clear on your strategy, and then design your organisation to support that strategy.

Ultimately, of course, it's customers that feed a business, but not just any old customers.

Enter Customer Quality Management

The purpose of this book is to bring focus back to the fundamentals of dealing with the people who will make your business stand or fall: the customers; to ensure you look at, see, and cultivate the *right* customers; and to bring home the message that selling is not something you can leave to the sales people.

Most sales management focuses on quantity, when it is quality that really matters:

Quality customers are customers who will add the most value to your business, whatever your business objectives are (profit, market share, turnover or whatever else they may be).

Quality interactions with your customers, and with the *right* people in the customer organisation, are interactions that build the relationships. People do business with people, and they do more business with people they like and who they believe are adding value to their lives, both business and personal.

Quality information about your customers is what you need to be able to add value in those interactions.

Quantity, so far from being good, can be very detrimental to your business.

 Myth 1: All customers are good customers

All too often we hear sales people say – "I treat all my customers the same!" or "The customer is king!"

It is a big, but very common, mistake to treat all customers equally. Most of the current crop of CRM tools either ignore key customer metrics or bury them in an avalanche of extraneous data. The key metrics for a customer are:

> How valuable are they to you?

> How valuable *could they be* to you?

> And hidden in these simple questions is another, crucial question: How do you define "valuable"?

All businesses have limited resources and face the challenge of getting the most out of what they have. To this end, your strategy must involve determining which customers are delivering the most value to your organisation, and which have the most potential to deliver value. The first group must be cared for and kept close; the second group must be nurtured and developed. As we will show in case studies throughout the book, Customer Quality Management (CQM) – paying close attention to the value to you, actual and potential, of your customers, rather than just looking at how many you have – yields dividends on a grand scale.

Defining "valuable" in your context is a necessary first step. Your business strategy may prioritise market share, revenue, or profitability. If you don't know what defines a valuable customer in terms of your strategic goals, you can't assess their relative worth to your business. Managing the quality of your customers is not to be disrespectful of any of them, but to recognise where value lies and prioritise accordingly.

Conventional sales training and sales management training typically fall short on four fronts:

Quantity wins over quality. The number of customers, number of orders (Strike rate), and number of sales calls are not a reliable measure of sales effectiveness. It's quality, not quantity, that will determine if you are going to grow your business.

Sales training stops with the sales people. Selling is not the function solely of the sales people. They are merely your front-line troops. Selling is the responsibility of every department and level in the organisation. Above all, though, it's the first-line management in sales that needs to be able to give strategic direction and coaching.

Sales goals are not put into the business' strategic context. Your sales effort has to be aligned to strategic goals, which in turn must be consonant with the available resources and the market opportunity.

Implementation is left as an exercise for the reader. Harried managers, under pressure to get results with a myriad demands on their time, all too often resort to sending the sales people on a course, or spending lots of money on yet another technological solution, or both, then waiting for results. Many training companies and software vendors are happy to oblige, to take the money and bid you God speed as they move on to the next sale.

Building sales and an understanding of Customer Quality Management require a company-wide culture shift, and making it stick requires more work on implementation and follow-up than on the initial training. Motivational talks and weekends away can do little more than fire people up to do the wrong things with more enthusiasm. Company vision has to be shared, bought into and lived.

CQM can produce spectacular results: case studies will tell of a PC distributor in a sluggish market achieving "85% growth year on year", of a banking division reporting "35% growth within 4 months", of a pharmaceuticals business entering the market with a generic drug six weeks after a directly competitive product – in a market where first mover advantage is taken as a given – and outselling the competitor by more than 10 times within 3 months.

Now for the bad news: CQM is not a quick fix. You cannot throw some money at it and wait for results, nor can you hope to achieve results in five minutes a day. The business books section in your local bookstore is crammed with business How-To's that have much in common with diet books: it's a lot easier to buy the books than to apply common sense, careful thought and some discipline. This is not the equivalent of some magic beans you can trade a cow for, throw on the ground, and then climb the beanstalk to the chest of gold.

What we will show you is:

- How to align what you have, what you want to achieve, and what the market needs.

- How to manage your customers in accordance with their value to you and your ability to serve them.

- How to enrol everyone in the organisation in a common sales strategy.

Chapter Summary – The Invisible Customer

Most businesses are surrounded by customers they just can't see, and are so busy chasing sales in the wrong places that they have no time for anything else. In short, they are not in control of their businesses: the customers are.

The key to regaining control of your business is to build a strategy around identifying, acquiring and keeping the right quality customers, by managing the quality of your interactions with them, through having quality information about them.

A systematic, scientific approach to Customer Quality Management will multiply the effectiveness of your sales force and deliver remarkable improvements in achieving your business goals, be it profit, market share or turnover growth.

Customer Quality Management

Customer Quality Management is about understanding which customers are most valuable to you, either currently or potentially, and shaping your organisation around securing or growing those customers.

In this chapter we talk about a customer's "value" in a general sense. It will often be measured as the profit you make from that customer, but profit is not always the measure you need. Your business strategy could call for maximising gross revenue or market share, for example.

An analysis of your customers and potential customers will show a mixture of results:

- High value customers, from whom you are getting a lot of business but with little scope for growth.

- High potential value customers, from whom you are getting a little business but could be getting a lot more.

- High potential value customers that you are not getting any business from.

- Medium to low potential value customers, from whom you may be getting some business but with limited growth potential.

- You will almost inevitably find you have customers who are costing you more to keep than you are getting or can hope to get from them.

Figure 1 illustrates this graphically.

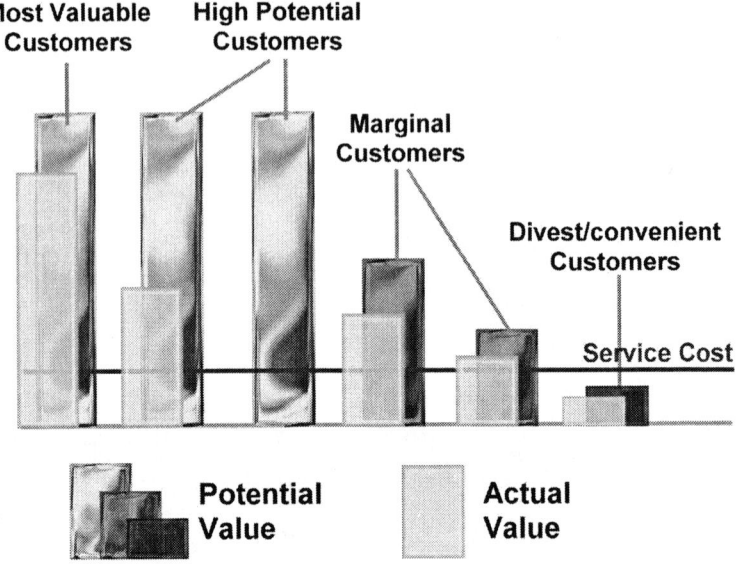

Figure 1: Customer Value

The 80/20 rule applies surprisingly often: 20% of your customers will be delivering 80% of the value. Indeed, it is not unusual to find even more skewed distributions, approaching 90/10. The same considerations will apply to your potential customers: of all the people you could be dealing with, a relatively small percentage will have the potential of the greatest returns. And yet, typically 80% of sales time is spent on the customers who bring in 20% of the profits.

 Myth 2: Last year's sales indicate this year's top customers.

If you follow this you may be proven right, but it is almost certain that last year's top customers do not represent the top *potential* for this year's business. Worse, this is a self-fulfilling prophecy that is at best a retention strategy to hold on to your current business rather than focusing on growing the business. It's thinking like this that makes your company's best potential customers invisible, sometimes even when you are already dealing with them. Some of your existing customers will be opportunity icebergs with only 10% of their potential visible to you.

Once you have an appreciation of the relative value and potential of your customers and prospects you can categorise them. We will use the labels Gold, Silver and Bronze, but the labels are not important as long as they are meaningful to you. You can call them A, B and C, or Premier, Special, and Standard, or 1, 2 and 3.

Using the Gold, Silver, Bronze labels, a few will be Lead – dead weights holding down your sales people and the organisation as a whole. It's not uncommon for some of the most serviced customers to turn out to be Lead: sales people get comfortable dealing with some customers, perhaps developing a close friendship with people in the customer organisation, resulting in a high frequency of contact and some bend-over-backwards deals.

Case Study

A company specialising in office filing systems, particularly for the medical market, was struggling to grow its profitability, even though sales were strong and the sales team were working flat out. All efforts to improve profits were boiling down to: work even harder. An analysis of the customer base showed that 50% of their accounts were not profitable. Most of their accounts were doctors: small practices with modest requirements. The sales team regarded them as their traditional market and were continuing to pursue more accounts with more doctors. As they acquired customers, they got busier but were not adding to the bottom line.

The solution was to stop dealing with the small accounts and divert them to wholesalers. Some accounts were lost, but this was not at a net cost in terms of profitability. In the meantime, the sales team were freed to focus on chasing down the bigger accounts: hospitals, clinics and medical aid societies. Within a year, profitability had doubled.

This is where simple measures of sales team performance like call rate are positively dangerous. **High call rates do not necessarily mean effective selling.** Calling on an unprofitable customer, so far from being positive, may generate higher volumes of unprofitable business.

Suppose you are in distribution of stationery, for example. You pride yourself on your high standards of service, and deliver all orders promptly. A customer who frequently orders half a dozen pencils, or a stapler, or a box of photocopy paper is costing you money on every order. Contacting that customer every week for the week's requirements is losing you money. Contacting them once every two or three months for a consolidated requirement might edge them into profitability for you: if you lose them because you don't call them often enough, you will save money. Of course, if you are targeting getting as many small businesses on board as possible with a view to later setting up small franchises as sub-distribution points, that could change your assessment completely.

Case Studies

Two examples from life will show how companies can fall into the trap of losing money on customers without even realising it:

An office stationery supplier found that 50% of their customers were doing less than $25 a month business with them, and yet they were delivering all orders, across the country. Not only were they losing money on these customers, but the drain on their resources (delivery vehicles and drivers, logistics and administration staff) was detracting from the level of service they were able to give to their profitable customers.

A finance house, financing business equipment, had sales people zealously chasing even the smallest deals. As an example, one sales person made two visits to a customer 60km (35 miles) away to conclude a finance deal on a laptop worth $1200. In addition, there were numerous phone calls and a dozen faxes required. As part of a bigger effort this could well make sense, but this was for a once-off deal for a small customer.

The level of service given to customers must be appropriate to their value to you. Airlines know this well: first class passengers get chauffer service, their own check-in, superior departure lounges, excellent food and wine, and additional deference from all the airline staff. Airlines have not all learnt how to handle the other end of the spectrum very well, but not many industries are so protected by massive barriers to entry that they can get away with shabby treatment of the low-value customers. Most businesses would do well to ensure that no customer is ever treated with disdain. You cannot afford to treat everyone like a king, but courtesy and respect are cheap and bring returns at all levels.

However, you cannot afford *not* to treat your Gold customers (and prospects) like kings and your Silver customers like lords. Running a business on a simple slogan like "Service Excellence", for example, leads to failure to take into account the different value of individual customers to your business. We will address later in this book the practical aspects of adjusting service levels to different customer levels.

Call Quality Management

 Myth 3: High call rates lead to high sales

Closely linked to CQM is Call Quality Management (CQM2). Simply measuring call rate without contextualising it against customer quality measures is dangerously inadequate, but introducing CQM on its own is not enough. A "call" can mean one of many kinds of contact with the customer. The quality of a customer call, which could be a meeting, a phone call, an email, a fax, or a social event, also needs to be tracked. What did the contact achieve, and what did it cost in time and money?

Without a means of tracking customer calls and recording the time and money expended, you will not know if you are allocating your resources properly in relation to the value you hope to derive.

CRM Software

Customer Relationship Management (CRM) software is often introduced as a tool to manage sales teams. As is common in today's hype-driven markets, the product description can sometimes exaggerate wildly: it is often designed to track transactions, and record encounters, with little attention paid to qualifying and quantifying the *relationship* aspect. Senior Management will generally believe that building relationships with customers is a Good Thing, so any software that is supposed to further that goal must likewise be a Good Thing.

The reality is that CRM software typically has shortcomings in managing both customer quality and call quality. CRM is a tool that can be used or misused. Automating customer relationships too often leads to a one-size-fits-all approach, and produces statistics that actually tell you very little about how much resource has been expended on which customers, and how that relates to the customers' potential value. Worse, CRM based on the wrong metrics can be a serious negative influence.

Suppose that you have successfully instigated a shift in corporate culture that is succeeding in getting the correct focus on both Customer Quality and Call Quality. There are few CRM packages that fit the CQM culture: introducing the wrong package can rapidly kill your initiative. The authority embedded in the method of working, metrics and reports of a CRM package can quickly overwhelm the culture you are trying to nurture. Much as children of immigrant parents will acquire the accents and attitudes of their schoolmates who they meet daily rather than continue in the way of their parents, when a sales team start using a CRM package the culture of the designers of the package is continually influencing the users. If your CRM package is not closely aligned with your strategy, your strategy will lose out to the drip-feed of the attitudes and assumptions built into the software. (See case study on p. 106.)

A national supplier of professional goods qualified its customers as A, B and C, and tracked call rates for each group. The sales team were measured on how many calls they made to 'A' customers.

However, on interrogating the sales team on what made 'A' customers, the answer was: it's the ones we can most easily get to see – which of course were also the ones that the competition could most easily get to see, and not correlated with the potential value of the customers. *(See the MedicSupply case study, p. 28)*

Be careful where you put the carrot! *(See Incentive Schemes, p. 59)*

Chapter Summary – Customer Quality Management

Customer Quality Management (CQM) means a new way of looking at customers, focusing on their *potential* value to your business, not what they are actually delivering to you. Implementing CQM will take a company wide culture shift from the sales people, through first-line and senior management to the support divisions.

Everyone needs to understand that some customers have more value or potential value than others, and that the level of servicing and attention that customers get must be based on their potential value to you. Low value customers must be cut, or handled in a way that demands few resources.

Sales people and their managers must break away from simplistic call counting and focus their attention on the quality as well as the quantity of their interactions with customers, and must aim to build relationships with their customers.

Do *not* let a CRM solution control your sales strategy. Your business processes will be what drives sales success. CRM should only support those processes, not drive them, and, wrongly implemented, can be destructive.

3

The Three Pillars of Business Strategy

Company Alignment

Many years ago in an old radio comedy show called *Take it from here* the dunce of the show, Ron, was asked by Eth, his girlfriend what he was making. "A handle for my portable, Eth" he replied. She asks, "Your portable what, Ron?" He answers "I don't know Eth, I've only made the handle so far."

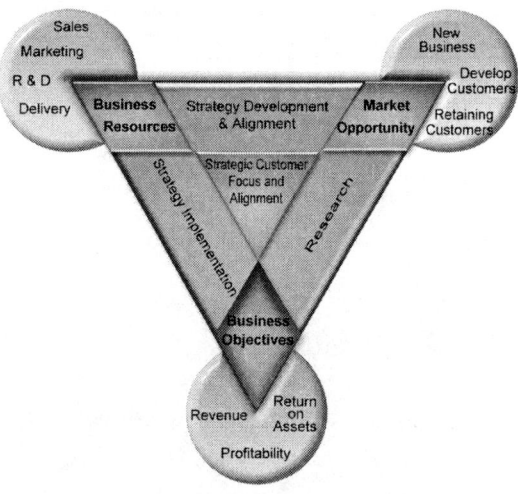

Figure 2: Company Alignment

It sounds silly, but there are companies that approach their business that way. They build pieces of the organisation without having a clear picture of what they want the whole to be.

A strategy for success builds on three pillars: what you want to achieve, what the market needs and what you have. Or to put it in more business-speak terms, business objectives, market opportunity, and business resources.

Your business objectives can be any combination of revenue, profitability and return on assets, or indeed other objectives such as brand building.

The market opportunity lies in understanding which markets and customers will deliver on your objectives: seeking new business, developing existing customers, and retaining customers. Retaining a customer is not the same as developing a customer: some customers can be grown into bigger customers; others need to be retained but do not have much potential for growth.

Business resources are the people and structures in place to handle sales, marketing, R&D, delivery (or logistics) and all the other business functions.

Three pillars standing alone are of little use. They must be built to support a common goal: your strategic customer focus. The key to a sound design is that all three must be aligned to a common purpose, and they must support each other.

 Myth 4: All Departments / Divisions work towards a common goal

Take business objectives as an example. Let's assume you are clear on what you want to achieve, and your primary goal is to gain market share and grow volumes. It isn't going to happen if your logistics and support team are focussing on excellent customer service and can't meet the increased volume of work. Conversely, if you are targeting high margin, niche markets that require specialist support and attention, but your delivery department is geared up for speed over cosseting, that also won't work. Neither approach from the logistics department is wrong *per se*, it's a question of whether it is suited to the customer base you are targeting. In some markets, a simple, efficient returns policy is considered excellent service ("If it doesn't work or you don't like it, bring it back for a refund"). In others, you need to focus on technical expertise ("If it doesn't work, our team of experts will find out why and sort it out for you").

As another example, suppose you identify an opportunity to develop new customers in a high potential market, but it requires some product re-development. If your R&D resources are inadequate, or are not focused on the right line of development, you will not develop that opportunity. Worse, and not an uncommon scenario, is where R&D is developing great products that will suit a tiny market niche where there is no money to be made.

All three legs influence one another. Market opportunity is something you cannot change, but you must make it your business (because it will make your business!) to understand where the opportunities lie for maximising your profitability. Business objectives you can review once you are clear on the market opportunity. Business resources you must adapt and align to the market opportunity, and generally, unless you are starting a green-field operation, will inform the business objectives you set.

The thread that should be becoming clear is alignment. The skill of architecting a business for maximum performance is in getting the business from top to bottom aligned toward a common strategy, and, most important, understanding how your customer focus fits that strategy.

Customerculture

Once you have defined your strategy and aligned business resources, business objectives and market opportunity, your next area to focus on is the "how". How are you going to build business with your customers?

Sales is a lot more than just the sales people getting the orders in.

Customers need to be cultivated, and we will emphasise that by coining the term *customerculture*, in the same vein as agriculture and viniculture. It's not an original analogy to talk of cultivating customers but it's one seldom properly explored, and even less often learned from. Many, if not most, businesses are still in hunter-gatherer mode: picking the low-hanging fruit from the trees in the forest, slaying the unwary buck, and eating today. Some have identified good hunting grounds where they can return regularly for fresh pickings, but they are at risk from changing circumstances: a new predator, a shift in migration patterns. They are not in control of their future.

Modern civilisation could not flourish until people developed agriculture to secure their food source, freeing them from the daily scramble to find food and freeing up resources to focus on higher goals. Businesses that are going to get the best from their resources need to have customerculture at the focus of their efforts.

In agriculture, success does not come from planting whatever seems a good idea at the time, nor can it be achieved by scattering seeds on a field and waiting for rain. A successful commercial farm pulls together market demand, planning and raw materials (seed, fertiliser, water), with constant care to adjust for the weather, disease, and predation from pests (and sometimes neighbouring farmers!).

Customerculture requires no less of a coordinated effort. When a farmer gets his crop in, it is the result of input of many kinds from a whole team of people, and the harvesting itself is just the culmination of a year's work. A business that is getting the most out of its customers is one that is doing all the things right that lead up to getting the orders. However, it's not enough to get everyone in the company to understand their roles in the sales process; you also have to get them to understand how to set priorities.

It's not unusual to get met with horrified indignation when you suggest that some customers should get treated differently from others. "We treat all our customers the same!" and "Every customer is important!" go the cries. Well, that does not make business sense. Certainly, no customer should be treated badly, but to devote the same amount of attention to every customer is not how you will get the most from your resources.

Think of customerculture again: if a farmer sees his crops faltering in a drought, but he does not have unlimited water available, which crops will get the water he does have? Clearly, the crop that is most valuable to him. It does not make sense to share the water equally amongst all the crops. Suppose the corn crop is worth $100,000 and the lucerne is worth $20,000, and sharing water equally means you will lose half of both, thus getting a total crop of $60,000. If you favour the corn, you might get 80% yield there, and only get 20% yield on the Lucerne – a total crop of $84,000.

> *Case Study*
>
> A pharmaceutical company had a simple call-scheduling approach for sales to pharmacies: they gave equal time to each of their customers. One chain, however, dominated the market in the target geographical area, having a 40% market share. Simply changing the priorities to allocate 40% of their sales time to the market dominator led to a rapid increase in business from them (and an increase in total business).
>
> Simple approaches like giving all customers equal treatment are indicative of either laziness in planning your sales strategy, or not having enough information about your customers to know which ones are the most important.

When you process orders, do they all go into a first-in, first-out queue? And your deliveries? It's very fair and even-handed, but it could mean, for example, that everyone gets a 2½-day turn-around from order to delivery. Now, in most companies, the 80/20 principle applies: 80% of your business comes from 20% of your customers. In fact, recent analysis at two client companies suggests that 85/15 or 90/10 is not unusual. If you introduce a fast-track order-processing and delivery system for the top 15% of your customers you will quite possibly be able to give them a 1 day turn-around, at the cost of the other 85% getting a 3-day turn-around. Bear in mind that your top customers are very likely ordering larger quantities, so the top 15% of your orders by value may well take only 5%-10% of the logistical and administrative effort to fulfil.

Perhaps you already do deliver 1-day turn-around to all your customers. What then would be the value to you of giving your top 15% half-day turn-around, and having a few of the rest of the deliveries stretch to a little over one day?

No company has limitless resources, nor are they delivering everything a customer could ask for in terms of reliability, speed, care and cosseting, but apportioning resources without fear or favour is not the solution.

Another example on the customerculture metaphor: if your prize bull is looking off-colour, do you leave him until his turn comes around in taking care of the rest of the herd, or do you summon the vet post-haste, knowing as you do that this bull is destined to sire dozens of high-yield cows?

Business Objectives

In ancient times, primitive sailors crossed vast tracts of ocean without sophisticated navigation equipment, motorised boats, or even much in the way of sails. We marvel at their achievements as archaeological evidence is uncovered showing what can be done just by drifting with the winds and tides. What the evidence does not show is the number who perished at sea as they drifted without direction, food or water.

A business that drifts without direction is not absolutely doomed to failure, but it is certainly well set to fail: the sea-bed of commerce is littered with the wrecks of businesses that drifted until they sank.

Business objectives give a business direction and goals against which to measure itself. You have to decide what constitutes success and how to determine if you are moving towards your goal or away from it, and then – the key message of this book – which customers are going to be the most important ones to you.

Defining Quality of Business

Quality can be a slippery concept until you get absolutely clear in your mind that it is not an absolute. Mostly when we use the term we use it in an implied context which hides the fact that quality is a measure of fitness for purpose, and if the purpose is not defined then the quality is not definable.

For example, if you say: "This is the best quality chocolate in the world!" you are implicitly saying that you believe that the majority of people who try it will give it top marks for taste, texture and colour. If on the other hand you say "This is the best oil in the world!" an engineer would look at you askance. Best for what? The best oil for your motor car engine is definitely not the best oil for the gearbox.

Quality of business has the same kind of ambiguity: it cannot be assessed without the context being clear, and that flows from clarifying your business objectives.

Types of Objectives

Business objectives generally fall into one of three categories: profitability, turnover, or market share, which may be qualified by a time-span. For example, you may be looking for customers with the potential to grow your market share over the next few years, or you may be looking to push turnover in the next 12 months.

It's outside the scope of this book to delve into when and why businesses should pursue different objectives: that's the subject of hundreds of books on business strategy. Companies have failed spectacularly in pursuit of objectives that, even if achieved, did not make for sustainable business, some notable examples of which appeared in the dot-com boom and bust. Our goal is to show businesses how to achieve their objectives as efficiently and effectively as possible. Setting the right objectives is a complete field on its own, but having the right objectives is not enough: you have to have every part of the business aligned towards those objectives. We will discuss alignment in more detail shortly.

Once you know your objectives, you can define your measures of customer quality through the process of determining Focus Factors, then measuring your customers against those factors (see p. 43, **Focus Factors**)

Market Opportunity

The more conventional way of looking at market opportunity is to ask the question "What need is there that my product or service can meet?" It is an important question, of course, but it is not very often that a business flounders because nobody wants its products: it's far more common for a business to be in trouble because it is not successful in selling its products.

The most important aspect of assessing market opportunity is to understand which customers will want your products, and which of those will generate the best returns for you (by whichever criteria you have set). When an oil company goes looking for oil, it doesn't drill holes randomly all over the landscape: it spends resources on identifying the areas where it is most likely to find oil and in the largest and easiest to exploit deposits. Your business must similarly be focused on identifying the most profitable areas to deploy your limited resources. Who, amongst your customers and prospects, can get you further towards achieving your vision? And who is holding you back rather than helping you advance?

Unprofitable customers can poison a business, and they can kill you with kindness. Think, for example, of a café in a shopping centre. If every table is occupied by regulars who linger for hours over a cup of coffee or two, the establishment is busy, with loyal customers, and likely to be short-lived. What it wants is businessmen in a hurry, eating at someone else's expense, who want a quality meal delivered and consumed quickly and price is a secondary consideration.

(We use the term unprofitable here in a general way to mean contributing less to you achieving your goal than they are costing you. If you were retired and wanting to run a café primarily to attract young, bright people to keep you feeling young yourself and in touch with the world, then a place full of artists and students might be just what you want. Alas, most businesses are out to make the best profit they can.)

Understanding your market opportunity means then being able to identify who your sales team, and indeed the whole organisation, should be focusing its attention on, and who it should **not** be focusing attention on.

Bad customers can be addictive. In fact, bad customers should carry a government health warning. Bad customers often come to you, are easy to deal with, and make you feel good, but they are not good for your business health.

Business Resources

Business resources are everything that goes to make up a business, but the most important view of your resources from a sales development perspective is as the organisational units that make up the business: sales, marketing, creditors, debtors, logistics, manufacturing, sales support, service, information technology, human resources, and any others you may have.

 Myth 5: Support departments will give top customers top service.

Support departments seldom know who the top customers are. They may know which customers generate the most work for them, but those are not necessarily the top (i.e. most valuable) customers. In fact, it's not uncommon for support departments to get an inverted view of who the most important customers are as the ones they deal with the most could be unprofitable customers that demand a lot of support (technical, logistical or administrative) for low returns. Perhaps more importantly, support people will rarely know the *potential* value of customers unless you make a particular effort to inform them.

Every department in the business *must* understand the business goals, the strategy for achieving those goals and the relative importance of different customers within that framework. A strategy can be killed by any department.

In one business, a growth strategy was set in motion with the target of achieving 25% increase in sales within 3 months. Manufacturing and purchasing planned for only a 5% growth in stock levels: at the end of the three months, sales had grown by 25% but they could not deliver, and the sales growth faltered and fell back. The problem was that the sales strategy was not communicated to the whole company, and the various support departments did not know the role they had to play.

Alignment

The interplay between Business Objectives, Market Opportunity and Business Resources is often circular: you can't generally fully define any of them without reference to the others. It's pointless wanting to be the biggest forestry business if you are based in the Sahara Desert. If your organisation's skills and resources are in growing trees, you must either relocate your business or switch to date farming.

In most cases, however, a company has resources that are mostly appropriate to the business objectives, and the objectives are not far out of synch with the market opportunities; but also in most cases the resources (people, systems, infrastructure and so on) are not aligned with the company's goals

If turnover is the goal, sales must be incentivised on turnover, not profits. If profit is the goal, then profit must be the yardstick – you can't expect your sales team to target high profits if they don't have the information they need nor rewards linked to achieving your company goals. And so on.

You have to communicate the priorities and the basis for categorising customers as Gold/Silver/Bronze to everyone, and structure their operations around those criteria.

The process of getting all parts of the organisation to understand and support the organisation's strategy and share a common view of the customers is what we call alignment. Examples of what goes wrong when you do not have alignment are abundant, and probably familiar to you. Here are some taken from life:

• Key customers were identified and the sales team briefed to grow the business from those customers. They were so successful that the credit department put a hold on the best customer's account because they had reached their credit limit. Because the creditors department were not involved in the key customer strategy, they were following "standard procedures" and in five minutes wiped out weeks of relationship and trust building.

- At a stage where it was managing for survival, a company brought in an operations manager whose brief was to contain costs. As the company stabilised and then started to target growth, the ops manager was still in survival mode, and sales efforts were continually hampered by lack of resources. He had not been brought into the process and re-oriented to the new strategy and priorities. Finally, the CEO realised what the problem was and brought in the ops manager for a discussion then told him to take a week's leave and come back with a new outlook. It worked, and in the weeks that followed the turnaround in sales and operational support was astonishing.

- The order processing in a company worked on linear, FIFO (first-in, first-out) basis: order received by sales, passed to order processing, then to despatch. It was an orderly, rigid procedure that treated all customers and all orders the same. It took no account of the fact that a hundred small orders could be worth far less than one large order from the bigger customers, yet clog up the entire logistics/despatch process, and a flurry of small orders could – and did – lead to orders for Gold customers being delayed. A fast track system for Gold customer orders was implemented, with everyone in the chain made aware of who the Gold customers were. Small orders were delayed marginally, but the big ones got priority treatment.

- A computer company aimed to increase its add-on business by offering an extended warranty on its laptops with a discounted spare battery bundled in the deal. The offer was supported by a card in the packaging and information on the web site, and customers were supposed to be able to take it up by telephone or email. Unfortunately, no-one thought to inform the telesales/fulfilment department, resulting in frustrated customers talking to or emailing call centre operators who did not know anything about the offer.

There are many other ways in which different departments can fail to work together. Is the research department developing something the market really wants? Does your credit application process put unnecessary hurdles in the way of new customers? Are your sales team letting people know who are the important customers and prospects, and why? Has management conveyed clearly to the sales and support departments, in terms meaningful to them, what the company is trying to achieve? Are the sales team trying to sell the products in quantities and with delivery schedules that are the most economical for Logistics to handle? Do the sales team know what products are available, out of stock, in short supply, or about to be launched? Has the receptionist been informed about the marketing campaign and the kind of enquiries it is likely to generate?

Achieving Alignment

Determining a vision and a strategy for an organisation needs to be followed by conveying those ideas to the managers of all the divisions in a three-step process:

1. Ensure all the managers understand the vision and the role their divisions have to play in achieving that vision. It needs to be clear that *everyone* is customer-driven.

2. Explain the basis for targeting customers and prospects, what criteria were used to categorise them as Gold, Silver

or Bronze, and how the sales team will be approaching their customer base. (See the section on **Focus Factors**, p. 43).

3. Brainstorm their ideas on how they can amend or improve their processes to support the sales strategy and deliver higher levels of service to Gold and Silver customers. Equally important is to generate ideas on what they can do to add value to the top customers (e.g.: phone them on their birthday, go on sales calls, send them information that will be of particular interest) and get them to commit to actions.

Here are some examples of how companies changed elements of their business following alignment discussions:

- In a finance company, the sales people would spend months courting a customer only to have the deal turned down when the paperwork was submitted to credit control. They changed their focus factors to include creditworthiness, and the credit department got involved in the pre-qualification of prospects and in visiting potential customers early in the sales cycle. The running average of 50% of new deals being turned down dropped to less than 20% rejections, cutting out wasted effort and reducing the number of people disgruntled by having their financing deals refused.

- A bank's business banking division had five sales teams who were too busy to get out and sell. All their time was taken up with office work and reactive selling. The administrative process was changed to offload the clerical work onto a sales support team, who also handled routine inbound calls from smaller clients. The sales people gained two hours a day for proactive selling, finding new, quality clients and spending more time on building relationships. Sales over the next six months increased by between 150% and 200% for each of the teams. The teams moved from being amongst the poorest in the organisation, to one of them becoming the top national team.

The message should be coming through clearly: the support divisions must be a part of, and party to, your strategy. Their operations and priorities have to be aligned with your sales objectives.

Achieving this alignment is not a once-off exercise: it requires constant management input, and the most important tool for this purpose is feedback. Your support team must be kept aware of the company targets and any changes in them, and must know the results being achieved. Success stories must be presented along with analysis of how the success was achieved and who contributed to it. This feedback is an essential part of implementing a strategy that needs people's mindsets to change.

The power of feedback to change how we think, act and even feel is seldom understood, but the fact is that regular, consistent feedback has an enormous influence. Studies have shown, for example, that people can exercise control over bodily functions that are usually regarded as involuntary, such as blood pressure and heart rate, simply by providing constant feedback. In one surprisingly simple experiment, subjects were shown a line on a TV screen that, unbeknown to them, represented their blood pressure, and were asked to concentrate on getting the line to move down. Amazingly, after an hour or two, they were indeed able to significantly lower their blood pressure – even though they were not even told what it was that the line represented.

The mind is able to exert an influence on the body in ways that the conscious mind is not aware of. An organisation can have a mind of its own and act in ways not intended, even to its own detriment. The organisational mind is influenced by constant feedback, and will in turn influence the organisation's systems to act in the desired way.

MediTrak Case Study

Background

MediTrak is a long-established company with over 60 years' experience in the health care industry mediating claims administration between health care providers (pharmacies, GPs, private and state hospitals) and medical aid societies. It is now primarily an IT company that has managed the transition from paper to electronic transactions and record-keeping. It is a dominant player in part of the market, with 95% of pharmacies on its books, and it owns the codification system used in the industry. However, market share with doctors was negligible.

The doctors' practices were variously still paper-based, or linked to their accounting systems, or using competitors' systems. MediTrak had a superior product but no outstanding edge to make a compelling case to switch. After three years of attempting to grow market share with the doctors there was little progress.

The sales effort had been built around three sales people supported by three technicians, casting the net wide by calling on as many doctors as possible.

The problem areas that were identified were:

- There was no sales manager to provide direction to the sales team.

- Sales and technical teams were not at all times aligned in their goals.

- The prospect database was too large, leading to poor Call Quality, and no attention being paid to Customer Quality. Out of some 9500 customers, 500 of them were accounting for just 0.5% of the business.

- As a result there was no targeting methodology in place to achieve sales growth.

Introducing CQM

The first step was to define sales objectives in terms of the basic business principles of CQM, namely the alignment of the available resources, the market opportunity, and the business objectives, and from there to identify the Focus Factors.

Focus factors are key in identifying the customers and prospects that have the most potential to contribute to the business' objectives and hence to provide the basis for categorising the customers and prospects as Gold, Silver or Bronze. The process of establishing the focus factors clarified for the sales team and support staff what their objectives should be.

With focus factors identified, the customer database was cut from several hundred per sales person to 150, and categorised within that as Gold, Silver or Bronze. The first focus factor identified was whether the prospect had either no computer system or an incompatible one, as this formed a large barrier to entry. Applying this immediately ruled out 70% of the current base, meaning that 70% of the sales effort had been spent on prospects with little chance of success.

MediTrak's solution is provided on a pay per claim basis, with no up front cost. Indiscriminate targeting meant many systems were installed and not used. To combat this, once a practice was identified as a Gold or Silver prospect, the influencers needed to be identified and won over. The sales teams were coached in building relationships: drawing up a contact frequency plan and developing different ways of making contact, on both personal and business levels.

Alignment of resources is a fundamental principle which

was addressed in many ways, such as:

- Technical implementation at the customer site can make or break a sale, so the sales/technical staff were formed into 4 teams of 1 sales + 1 technical (a fourth sales person and technician were added), who worked as a team and were recognised as a team.

- The call centre operators were given a list of the Gold customers and a fast track for handling Gold calls was put in place.

- The sales team were supplied with a list of the support and input they could expect from management for each category of customer; for example, writing letters of appreciation, attending functions.

The implementation was supported by introducing Tracer CQM software to assist the sales team with managing their database and keeping track of their objectives. Meanwhile, recruitment of a sales manager was in progress.

Results

Six months into implementation of CQM, sales to doctors had increased fourfold, against an expected increase based on historical performance of 20%-30%.

A sales manager was appointed, who further analysed the customer base and cut it again to a maximum of 80 per sales team. Now, a three-year history of selling to doctors as a loss leader has been turned into a profitable sector.

Summary

- The process at MediTrak followed the basic principles of CQM by first asking basic questions:

- What are the business objectives?

  o Why? Market share? Profitability? Long term goals?

- Where is the market opportunity?

- o Apply 80/20 rules

- o 80% of your return (or potential return) will be from 20% of your customers/prospects

- o 80% of your sales effort should be focused on 20% of your customers.

- Apply focus factors to qualify your database (see Chapter 4, Focus Factors, p. 43)

- How do we align the business resources behind our objectives?

Once answers to the questions had been formulated, they proceeded to act on the information:

- Generate strategies to address Gold and Silver clients and prospects

- Draw up a contact frequency plan, paying attention to number, variety and quality of contacts.

- Devise ways to add value to customers with every contact.

Chapter Summary – The Three Pillars of Business Strategy

A successful business strategy is built on three pillars:

- Business objectives. These could be any combination of profit, turnover, and market share, and possibly others.

- Market opportunity, defined not only in terms of products and services but also in terms of who the best customers are.

- Business resources. These comprise your people (in all the different departments), buildings, plant, systems, finance.

The key to a successful strategic design is that all three pillars must be aligned to a common purpose and they must support each other.

4 Preparing for Customer Quality Management

There are at heart only two principles that underlie everything in this book:

1. The 80/20 rule: 80% of your business comes from 20% of your customers. The exact split will vary: in some cases it can be as extreme as 90% or more of the business coming from 10% of your customers, but the principle remains. Businesses usually spend the bulk of their resources on the customers who contribute the minority of the value to the business.

2. Business is about relationships. People do business with people, and if you can add value to someone's life (business or personal), that person will want to do business with you.

Customer quality management is about identifying who your quality customers (and prospects) are, and building quality relationships with them. When you know who your important customers are, then you can start apportioning your time appropriately. This is the subject of this chapter.

Understanding that quality customers make for a successful business is the first step you have to take, but once you take that step your next thought will likely be: how do we go about putting this into practice? That will be addressed in Chapter 8.

Defining Quality

Quality is at times an elusive concept: we all think we know what it means, but when you start to use it as an objective measure, context becomes a key factor. What constitutes quality in one context does not necessarily work in another. Good quality apples for eating fresh are different from the best for cooking (good eating apples are too sweet and soft for cooking). A great acting performance for a Shakespearean tragedy on stage would appear heavy and over-the-top for a TV sitcom.

Defining quality of customers is every bit as elusive if you do not have the criteria clearly defined. In *Company Alignment* we looked at aligning business resources, business objectives and market opportunity, the three pillars on which to build your customer strategy. In considering market opportunity, we looked at the need to classify opportunities as Gold, Silver, or Bronze (or whatever similar terminology works best for you). Before you can implement CQM, you have to have your quality measures appropriately specified: if you can't measure quality you certainly can't manage it.

What makes a quality customer?

 Myth 6: Last year's top customers should be this year's top customers

Bad measures of customer quality are common, and the commonest of all is to let history be your guide. When the basics of CQM are being taught in a company, and sales people and their managers are asked "Who should your Gold customers be? Who should be on your 'A' list?" the almost invariable response is to pull out the sales for the last 12 months and select the top 10 or 20 customers.

This is wrong on several counts.

- Top revenue does not necessarily mean top profitability, nor top market share.

- Your business objectives may not be the same as they were 12 months ago. The business environment changes, products evolve, competitors come into play, and a host of factors could be changing what you need from your customer base.

- Your relationship with your top customers may be so strong and well-established that you are getting as much business as you can hope for from them. Focusing on them again this year will at best be a retention strategy if there is no room for growth.

- **The customers you don't have, who could be extremely valuable to you, are not on this list!**

The first step then in implementing CQM is to determine a set of Focus Factors: the criteria you will use to assess the actual and potential value *to your business* of customers.

Focus Factors

Focus factors are factors identified by both senior management and sales people, with input from support functions, to help determine what qualifies a customer as Gold, Silver or Bronze.

Senior management must be involved to ensure that the factors are consonant with the company's vision and are consistent with the strategy.

Sales people must be involved so they understand the basis for setting the focus factors and can translate strategy into practical customer targeting.

Market research is very important in developing focus factors. It brings an element of objectivity into the process and helps to identify potential business by product and location. Miners looking for real gold and silver do extensive research to identify where the richest mineral veins are likely to be before they start investing huge efforts in digging. Market research is like conducting a geological survey to identify mineral deposits so you know where to focus your efforts.

Lastly, support functions should be involved in determining focus factors. In the case mentioned earlier of the finance company (under *Achieving Alignment* on p. 32), where prospects cultivated over 6 months were turned down at the final hurdle by credit control, including credit control in finalising the focus factors would have avoided embarrassment and wasted effort. Neither sales nor management can be expected to be aware of all the factors throughout the organisation that can affect the viability or profitability of a given customer.

There is no one set of focus factors for an industry or market area, nor even necessarily for an organisation. Different departments or sections of your organisation could have quite different measures. A pharmaceutical company could have different strategies for selling to hospital chains, government health departments and retail pharmacies. Focus factors will typically vary with the sales team (channel, direct, telesales), territory, and at different levels in the organisation. Management, just as much as sales, needs to prioritise customers, but what constitutes an 'A' customer to a telesales agent is not likely to be an 'A' customer to a board member.

You must also never forget that selling is not a function limited to sales people. Every department plays a role in the sales effort. Logistics, finance, technical support, marketing – all have to have clear in their minds which customers are key. One of the risk factors in outsourcing functions such as logistics is the difficulty of communicating your priorities to the service provider if a one-size-fits-all approach is not suited to your market (and it seldom is).

Focus factor examples are:

- Revenue potential
- Influence on other customers
- Geographical location
- Market share
- Return on Equity
- Payment history
- Quality of staff (in the customer organisation)

Table 1: Channel Sales Focus Factors

Factor 1	Annual Turnover Potential
Gold	$5 mil +
Silver	$3m to $5m
Bronze	$1m to $3m
Factor 2	**Profitability (GP %)**
Gold	15% +
Silver	12 % to 15%
Bronze	10% to 12%
Factor 3	**Annual Gross Profit**
Gold	**Potential**
Silver	$750 000 +
Bronze	$550 000 to $750 000
	$355 000 to $550 000
Factor 4	**Debtor Days**
Gold	Less than 50
Silver	50 to 65
Bronze	60 +
Factor 5	**Number of sales people**
Gold	5 +
Silver	3 to 5
Bronze	1 to 3

Table 1 illustrates possible focus factors for a distribution company in the computer industry for assessing its channel partners. These factors can be used in combination to rank customers as Gold, Silver or Bronze.

The same organisation could also have a sales team targeting retail stores, and their focus factors would be different. Table 2 illustrates a possible set of Focus Factors for sales through retail stores.

As a further example, Table 3: Business-to-Business Focus Factors gives an example of focus factors that were developed for a corporation seeking to do business with other corporations.

Table 2: Retail Sales Focus Factors

Factor 1	Turnover Potential
Gold	A Stores
Silver	B Stores
Bronze	C Stores
Factor 2	**Profitability**
Gold	13% +
Silver	12% to 13%
Bronze	11% to 12%
Factor 3	**Professional / Motivated / Dynamic people in the Store**
Gold	Highly Professional/Motivated and Dynamic
Silver	Highly Professional and Motivated
Bronze	Professional
Factor 4 Gold	**Internal Processes in the Store to Influence Sales** Both the Store Manager and the Sales people are able to influence sales
Silver	The Store Manager will dictate which product will be pushed
Bronze	The Sales people can decide which product they will push
Factor 5	**Product knowledge development in Stores**
Gold	Excited to Improve their Product Knowledge
Silver	Open for Product Knowledge training
Bronze	Reluctant to improve their Product Knowledge
Factor 6	**Internal Marketing strategies and initiatives**
Gold	Guaranteed Promotional opportunities
Silver	Guidance Necessary for Promotional Opportunities
Bronze	Reluctant to allow Promotional Opportunities

Focus factors will vary with industry, market segment, and, most importantly, with the business objectives of the organisation or department. It is perfectly possible for two businesses selling competitive products into the same market to have very different focus factors.

Proper selection of focus factors is critical to the success of the scoring. If we stay with the example of the computer industry, a small consultancy that gives you very little business but asks a lot of very technical questions that use up sales and support time may be recommending equipment to a top 100 company. You cannot afford to divest yourself of such a customer!

Focus factors are **not** a scorecard. They do not provide a mechanical tick-the-boxes-and-add-the-points assessment of customers; they are a decision support tool to help focus thinking (which is why they are called focus factors).

Targeting on weighted sums can give you wrong results. For example, one targeting approach tells you to identify high profit/high turnover businesses – but what if the business you identify has just purchased a competitors solution? Or is in a city where you have no representation?

Averages are dangerous things, with more power to mislead than most people imagine. Imagine you are standing with one foot on an ice block and the other in scalding water. On average, you should be comfortable! Or take a more subtle example: if on a long trip you travel half the distance at 120kph and half the distance at 60kph, your average speed is not 90kph, it's 80kph. Time spent on poor quality customers will similarly drag down your overall sales performance more than you expect.

Focus factors should be used to quantify customer potential and clarify your view of the customer. Then, based on an overview of the ratings for that customer, you classify the customer appropriately. In general, complex scoring or averaging systems are not appropriate: it's quite possible for a significant score on one factor to outweigh all the others, positively or negatively.

Table 3: Business-to-Business Focus Factors

Factor 1	Turnover Potential
Gold	$150m +
Silver	$100m to $150m
Bronze	$50m to $100m
Factor 2	Strategic Fit (Top 300 Corporates)
Gold	Listed
Silver	Large Corporate
Bronze	Medium Corporate
Factor 3	Profitability
Gold	10% +
Silver	8% to 10%
Bronze	5% to8%
Factor 4	Progressive and advancing Corporates
Gold	Fast growing industry e.g. Telecommunication
Silver	Medium paced industry e.g. Banking
Bronze	Declining industry
Factor 5	Financial Professionalism
Gold	Pays within 30 days from invoice
Silver	Pays between 30 and 45 days
Bronze	Pays slower than 45 days
Factor 6	Serviceability (Km from depot)
Gold	Less than 10 Km
Silver	10 Km to 30Km
Bronze	Further than 30 Km

It's also important to appreciate how certain factors can have a disproportionately small or large influence. Attempting to score factors mechanically can lead to completely incorrect results. Small components in a large mix can have a disproportionate effect, either disproportionately small or disproportionately large. For example, suppose you have two buckets, one filled with ice cream and the other filled with

> How many customers can a salesperson handle? There is no one answer to that question, as it varies with the market, nature of goods and services, and your route to market: direct sales will typically allow a higher ratio than channel sales, for example. As a rough guide you can use the following: when selling to:
>
> | | |
> |---|---|
> | Individuals: | 200 |
> | Small companies: | 120 - 150 |
> | Large businesses: | 40 - 60 |
> | Channel: | 20 - 30 |

horse manure. Take a spoonful of each and mix it into the other. The horse manure is not improved in the slightest by the admixture, but the ice cream is totally ruined.

In some situations you may have factors rated Lead. The Bronze criteria normally define a cut-off point – lower than Bronze would mean that that customer is not a target – but it can help to define explicit Lead criteria. These are customers who have a 'horse manure' factor that no amount of ice cream can counterbalance. If you have done your assessment correctly, no alchemy will be able to transform Lead customers into Gold, let alone Bronze or Silver, as these are customers who are costing you money or are otherwise damaging your pursuit of your vision and have no potential to become valuable. These are customers you need to divest yourself of; or at best, devise ways of handling such that they do not cost you more than they are worth either in direct costs or in opportunity costs. **Time spent on a marginally profitable customer with no potential for improvement is time you no longer have to invest in your more valuable customers.**

Too much or not enough Gold

As a rule of thumb, your scoring should leave you with roughly 20% Gold customers, 30% Silver and 50% Bronze. A quick check is to rank all your customers and examine the top 20% as your probable Golds. Review the list against your focus factor evaluation and see if your experience and knowledge of your customers agrees with

So what do you do if you have too few Gold customers, or too many?

If you have too few, the first thing to check is that you have included all your possible Gold customers. It's normal in a first pass exercise to overlook *potential* high-value customers, whether new or existing. If you feel you have covered those bases, then you may need to go out looking for more potential Golds.

What do you do if your scoring leaves you with twice as many customers in the Gold, Silver or Bronze category as your sales team are capable of servicing properly? If that's the case, and you cannot increase your available resources, then you must adjust the criteria and re-score until you are down to manageable numbers. Perhaps you will set up a telesales department to deal with the customers who no longer make the grade, devise a new strategy for them, and re-rate them with a new set of focus factors.

In one case (see the MedicSupply case study below), proper scoring of the customer base resulted in over 4000 customers being taken off the regular visit list and transferred to a telesales-only operation. In this case, implementation of CQM resulted in 85% growth in sales in the first year.

Identifying focus market segments

Many businesses operate in more than one market segment. The same principles that are used to identify your Gold, Silver or

Bronze clients can and should be applied to identify the market segments with the greatest potential, and **then** to identify the right customers in those segments.

 Myth 7: Sales people target customers who are best for the company.

People generally act in a way that rewards them most, or punishes them least, and often let the short-term override the long-term. Sales people are no different from anyone else in this respect. They will target customers according to their own needs, not the company's, and in many instances will opt for the easiest short-term options. The surest indications of how a sales team will focus their efforts are how they are measured and rewarded (see **Incentive Schemes** in Chapter 10).

The case study that follows is an example of how changing the criteria for performance measurement of the sales team: specifically, changing the criteria for the customers they had to target most strongly, dramatically improved sales.

Case study: MedicSupply

We will call the company MedicSupply.

MedicSupply had a customer rating system that rated customers as A, B or C. Call rates were set based on the customer rating. 'C' customers were those that required a country trip. Although not at first obvious, a little analysis soon made it clear that effectively the ratings came down to:

A: Easy to call on

B: Hard to call on

C: Country trip

B customers, being hard to call on, did not yield a lot of business, so were not called on often– the circularity of the rating became self-evident. B customers were typically hard to call on because they were very busy practices, or run by doctors not interested in socialising and slow to change, or both. However, once you start to look at the criteria for defining high potential customers these are the very characteristics you look for.

MedicSupply went back to the drawing board to develop a set of focus factors to re-define their A, B and C categories. 'A' customers were the big groups that placed larger consolidated orders. Over the following months the sales team were focused on building up relationships and trust, targeting new A and B customers. A marketing campaign targeted the smaller pharmacies and practices.

The effectiveness of the new sales focus was put to the test after a few months when MedicSupply launched a new generic product.

A product launch typically involved the sales people going to see all their customers to tell them about the product. In this case, they had their customer base clearly defined, and were able to see all their Gold customers – 80% of their business potential – in the first week. Further, the time invested in the months prior to the new product launch had strengthened relationships to such a degree that many of their top customers trusted the sales representatives, wanted to help them, and wanted to give them the business. When they were advised of the pending release of the new product many of them actually held back ordering competitive product until the release because they wanted to give the business to MedicSupply.

In the pharmaceutical market where generics are concerned it's taken as a given that first to market has a huge advantage. In this case, MedicSupply were 6 weeks behind the competition. The competitor had sold $5000 worth of their product in the first 6 weeks: in the next 6 weeks, MedicSupply achieved sales of $650,000 with their product, far exceeding expectations and annihilating the competitor's first-to-market advantage.

This case incidentally also highlights the importance of involving support functions in the entire sales process: when customers are willing to delay orders so they can place them with you, you cannot break that trust by not delivering on time.

An objection sometimes raised is that more business from fewer customers makes for lower administrative costs but brings higher risk. Good planning, ensuring the entire company is on board to give Gold customers top service, and getting your sales team out looking for more Gold customers are your risk management plan. It's a mistake to think there is safety in numbers if the numbers you are talking about are large numbers of unprofitable or marginally profitable customers.

The Second Dimension

So far, we have talked only of rating customers in terms of their value to you (whether actual or potential). The second dimension is the categorisation by the stage of sales development you are in with each customer. This puts customers into one of four groups:

Potential: Someone you think may be a worthwhile customer.

Attract: A qualified potential customer who is not currently giving you business.

Expand: Current customer who is giving you only part of his business.

Sustain: Current customer who is giving you all or nearly all of his business.

Figure 3: Customer Assessment Grid shows the final customer assessment grid, which is the base on which CQM is built.

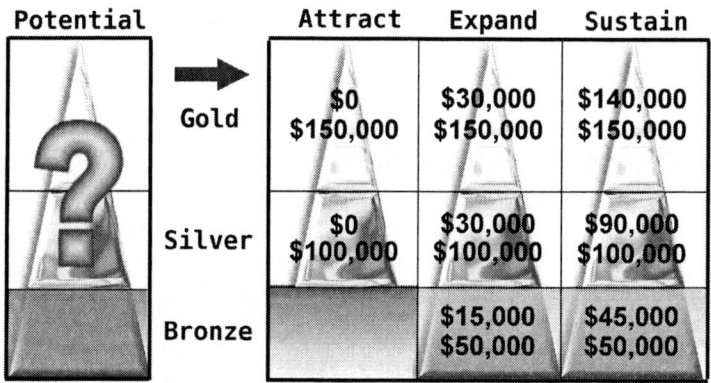

Figure 3: Customer Assessment Grid

In Figure 3 we have for illustration supposed that a Gold customer is one who can bring you $150,000+ worth of business, Silver is $100,000 – $150,000, and Bronze is $50,000 – $100,000. The pairs of numbers in each block are the actual business from that customer (upper figure), and the potential business (lower figure).

So for example, a Gold Attract customer is one with whom you are doing no business at present but potentially you believe is worth $150,000. You want to attract that customer because he can be developed through the stages of Expand (you are now getting some of his business) to Sustain (you are getting most or all of his business). A Silver Sustain is one where, for example, you are currently getting $90,000 out of a possible $100,000.

The key mindset shift is to *target according to **potential** business*, and to understand that developing a customer means to realise the potential.

For this targeting to be accurate, you must know enough about your customer to know what the potential is. Rating a customer according to the business they place with you can be a big error: a customer may place limited business with you because they are testing you first; or they may have a policy of spreading their risk by spreading their purchases, a policy which you may be able to alter by delivering above expectations. Quality information about your customer means that when you get the first bit of business from a Gold Attract customer, everyone who deals with that customer in any way must be made aware of the customer's status and treat him accordingly.

With the right focus factors, a Gold customer is a Gold customer *regardless of how much business they are actually giving you*. A Bronze customer **cannot** be developed into a Silver or a Gold – their status may change because of external factors, but never as a result of your sales efforts. By definition, a Bronze customer is one with limited potential, and at best you can develop that customer to realise the maximum possible business from him, but he will still be a Bronze.

It's worth recapping the significance of the different areas in the grid.

Potential: possible customers who still need to be qualified. You should be qualifying them to identify Gold and Silver prospects.

Attract: prospective customers who have been qualified. You should only be actively targeting Gold and Silver potential.

Expand: existing customers who are not giving you most of their business, but potentially could be developed into loyal customers. Gold, Silver and Bronze is a measure of their *potential* value to you.

Sustain: existing customers who are giving you most of their business. Gold, Silver and Bronze is a measure of their *actual* value to you.

If you have targeted your customers correctly, you will be moving them through the spectrum from Potential to Attract, then Develop, then Sustain. Notice in particular the block for Bronze Attract: it is blanked out.

You should never have a customer rated as Bronze Attract because Bronze customers are customers who come to you or are inherited from past sales efforts. They must be treated decently and efficiently, unless they are actually losing you money, in which case you must change your rules to prevent that continuing. You might for example institute a minimum order value policy, or put an order handling or delivery charge on small orders. With care, you may well retain marginal customers and turn them into mildly profitable ones, but whatever you do you cannot lavish the same attention on them that you give to your Gold and Silver customers. If you are spending your efforts on attracting Bronze customers you are wasting resources that would be better spent on acquiring, expanding and sustaining Gold and Silver customers.

You will have current customers who do not make the grade even to Bronze status. **Sales people should never deal with these customers.** A separate, purely reactive strategy – perhaps a call centre – should be put in place for these. However, your reactive strategy must include checks and escalation mechanisms to pick up potential high-value customers to ensure they do not get mired in a call centre or telesales process. Existing low-value customers can suddenly become high-value customers as they land a key contract, or a high-potential prospect you have not yet identified can end up with telesales.

Your strategy has to be prepared for this, which means providing the right processes and incentives for your reaction team. For example, simply incentivising a telesales team based on total sales will encourage them to hold on to customers as long as they can, which could be the worst thing to do.

Another risk you must take into account is that elevating certain customers to Gold or Silver status may lead to Bronze customers being alienated. Part of the implementation challenge is to ensure that the change in status of these customers is handled carefully and diplomatically. But, when the chips are down, you are better off losing some Bronze customers than failing to retain a Gold customer.

A case study from the office equipment rental business.

The company's business was the selling of rental agreements for office equipment: PCs, printers, multi-function devices, and the like. Their customers ranged from one-man businesses to large corporations.

The company had been in business for many years and had built a reputation and a customer base. The sales team were busy, working flat out just dealing with unsolicited enquiries, and nearly everyone thought business was booming. Top management, though, saw that the business was not growing. The fact was that they were not in control of their business: it was the customers who were driving the business. In all the frantic activity, the sales team had lost sight of the fact that spending one to two days organising the rental of a single PC was not a good use of their time. Being busy had become a status symbol, an end in itself. The company was driven by reactive selling instead of proactive targeting.

An analysis of the sales showed that 7% of the customers were generating 90% of the business. The business was not growing because 93% of the customers were taking up 90% of the company resources to generate 10% of the business. No-one had time to think about getting more, and better, customers.

The sales team of five was working on an "everybody does everything" basis. The first step in restructuring the business was to pick one of the five who had the strongest office administration bent and assign her to handle all incoming sales. The immediate objection was "I can't handle all the incoming calls!", which was dealt with by streamlining the process as much as possible, then politely telling those customers who could not be accommodated that the company was unable to handle their enquiry for the moment. It had to be accepted that some sales would be lost, though the telesales person had to be able to recognise high potential customers and pass them on to one of the account managers. A cap was set on the size of contract that could be handled by telesales, and account managers had a floor below which they had to pass the customer on to telesales. The telesales person ended up with more than enough business to be able to selective and ended up achieving higher sales (and commission) than before.

In the meantime, the remaining four sales people suddenly had time to start proactively targeting new business and were out selling again.

In one year, sales grew 450% with no additional sales staff and nobody having to work any harder.

The questions a sales manager has to answer are: Who is in control? You, or your customers? Are you letting your customers dictate how successful you are going to be? If every initiative is met by cries of "We're too busy" or "We can't do that, we don't have time" then you are not in control, you are reacting to events like a cork on the waves in a storm.

Separate the Urgent from the Important

The perennial curse of time management is separating the urgent from the important. Mostly, urgent matters arise from errors, poor delegation, difficult customers, and generally Things Going Wrong. They will always swamp the important if you let them. Important matters are related to your vision and overall strategy.

 Myth 8: Busy salespeople are an indicator of sales.

It's easier to let yourself be driven by responding to urgencies: it requires no planning or strategic decision-making, and creates a feeling of being usefully busy. In general, though, attending to the current urgent issues will have little or no impact on reducing the number of urgent issues that will crop up in future.

Important work must be planned such that the urgent work can flow around it. Think of your time as a bucket into which you have to fit blocks (the important work) and sand (the urgent work). If you put all the sand in first you won't be able to fit many blocks in; but if you put the blocks in first you can pour the sand around and between the blocks.

Important work is an *investment* of your time; urgent work is an *expenditure* of your time. Important works towards your vision; urgent just keeps you busy.

Urgent matters that eat into your productive time are everywhere: reports; meetings; handling customers who should never have come to you; spending time on unprofitable but demanding customers.

Important matters are ones like: spending time on understanding who are the right customers; generating proactive ideas for frequent contact with those customers; ensuring your contacts add value to your customer; developing and properly using internal and external resources. The important activities must lead your strategy and chime with your ability to execute.

Strategy must **always be** subordinated to your vision lest it become the end in itself. Your strategy can be to look for value, but if you do not know clearly what constitutes value and how to recognise it your search will be inefficient at best. Flea markets are full of people pawing through tables of bric-a-brac looking for something of value, when the real value could be a dusty old Rembrandt stored in the attic at home. A directed, informed search for value comes from paying attention to the important.

Multi-Level Selling

Picking focus factors and developing a customer assessment grid is not a once-off exercise. We have mentioned already that different departments or sales teams may pick different factors for their assessment grid. A company may have a high-level strategy which will lead to a Gold/Silver/Bronze ranking used by senior management, but a small regional office will have its own criteria for its own view of the market, with its own set of customers and focus factors, possibly a different product set, and hence its own assessment grid.

Localised assessments must nonetheless mesh with company goals so that sales people will have a correct expectation of the level of support they will get from the rest of the company. A customer that is rated Gold for a given sales person or team must get Gold treatment from everyone in the company who deals with that customer. This does not necessarily mean that all Gold customers get the same level of service: Gold service as defined for a telesales customer is not the same as Gold service as defined for a strategic account. However, appropriate levels of service for different types of customer must be understood and communicated to all sectors of the business. Mismatches here will nullify your strategy. Nothing discourages a sales person as much as one of her star customers that she has been cultivating for months being given second-rate treatment by the rest of the company.

On the other hand the organisation as whole must recognise that sometimes localised goals will necessitate localised focus factors and a localised realignment of resources. Localised in this context may mean geographically localised, or based on some other market segmentation criterion.

When dealing with a large customer it may make sense to separately assess the people within the customer organisation along strategic and operational lines. Separate analyses, typically along influence lines, will guide the senior management working at the strategy level and the account managers working at the operational level. It is not unusual to see companies neglecting to address both. When that happens, you get the client's management endorsing your company but the buyers and users go their own way; or the client's operational team want your product but are overridden by policy decisions.

Identifying the Business Influencers

The grid in *Figure 3: Customer Assessment Grid* is equally effective for assessing the business influencers in your client's organisation. Gold, Silver or Bronze will indicate very influential, somewhat influential, or having a little influence. Attract, Expand and Sustain will indicate your relationship with that person.

Attract means you do not currently have a close relationship. The person is either actively opposed to you, or is disposed to a competitor.

Expand means the relationship is neutral or there is some trust and warmth, but it could be better.

Sustain indicates a stable, close relationship that needs to be maintained.

Prospect refers to those people who are unknowns to you. You don't know their possible influence, nor where they stand with respect to you and whatever you are selling.

Analysing your client organisation's business influencers and your relationship with them is a strong indicator of where you are headed with that client. For example, if you identify one or more Gold influencers where the relationship is at the Attract stage, you have a problem and your business with that customer is at risk. If you don't have the relationship with a major influencer, your competition might.

Understanding Business Influencers

To buy or not to buy – that is the question that your customers are asking themselves, and the decision-making process can be as full of characters and plot twists as any Shakespearean tragedy. Like it or not, it is an essential part of sales strategy to understand and identify the players.

Figure 4: Business Influencers illustrates the principle characters in the sales plot.

The Guide: The Guide can be your pilot, who helps navigate you through the challenges of your business relationship with your client organisation. The Guide will feed you information such as the company's goals and objectives, historical influences, company culture, the current internal attitude towards your company and products, and the politics: promotions, demotions, departures and alliances. The guide can help you position your product or service to best fit the client needs, and help you identify who are the Gold and Silver business influencers.

The Veto Power: Usually found at the top of the organisation or business unit, this is the person that will take the final decision or has veto power. It's normally the CEO or Managing Director, but could be delegated to a functional or department head.

The Affected: The Affected are the people that will be affected by using your product or service. They will assess how well your product will fit into their company and what other benefits will be received or mutually profitable synergies established by working with your company. This is where "The rubber meets the road".

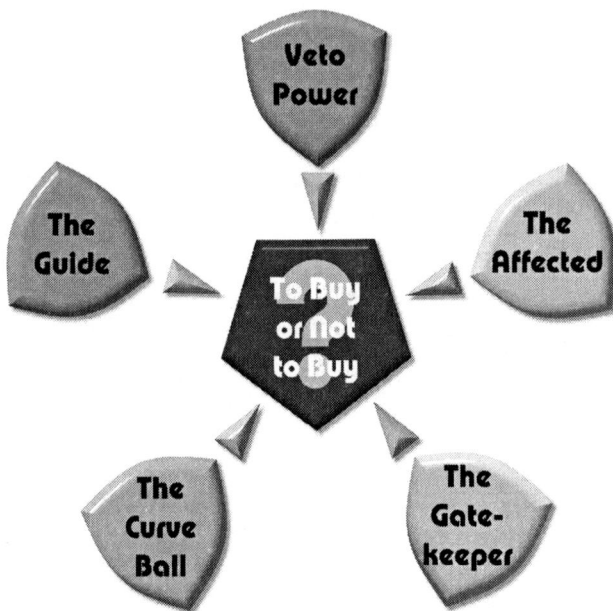

Figure 4: Business Influencers

The Gatekeeper: The Gatekeeper is the person(s) who can specify, set standards and criteria or see that what you sell will fit their company. They are there to check the fine details to protect the company. They are often the restraining arm of the company preventing access and can be anyone ranging from receptionists (first-line of defence) to financial directors.

The Curve Ball: This is any person, situation or even another company that has an influence on any or all of the Business Influencers that may ultimately affect whether you get the business or not. Many a deal has been derailed by something that never even showed on the sales person's radar. You have to be alert for unexpected and unconventional threats. It is here that good personal relationships can be invaluable: informal, not-directly-business discussions that range far and wide are more likely to give you an insight to the influences that can appear from unexpected quarters.

Very large client organisations will need to be further broken up for analysis by division or department. It's rare that one selling strategy will be the best for every part of a massive corporation.

We will return to the subject of business influencers in Chapter 6 as we get into determining call frequencies and ways of adding value to sales contacts, but for now, keep this simple maxim in mind: if it influences your business, it *is* your business.

Chapter Summary – Preparing for Customer Quality Management

Your top customer for the coming year may well not be your top customer from last year. If you want to grow your sales you must systematically set about identifying your top customers by *potential*.

- Identify the markets you want to attack through developing focus factors.

- Use focus factors to identify the top customers with the highest potential return.

- Identify your top current customers that you need to keep and develop.

Once you have a segmentation and have classified your customers into your Gold, Silver and Bronze customers, develop strategies to *attract* new high-value customers, *expand* existing customers with high potential but lesser actual value, and *sustain* customers who are valuable and giving you most of their potential business.

Understand the different business influencers you will have to deal with: the Guide, the Veto Power, the Affected, the Gatekeeper, and the Curve Ball.

Building Relationships in a CQM Environment

Sales Conversion Rate: Frequent Contact Works

The Numbers Game

The more tickets you buy in the lottery, the more likely you are to win. It's a simple, obvious truth, isn't it? Unfortunately, though, it's at best misleading and sometimes downright wrong.

Every now and then the papers publish some interesting facts about the numbers people choose, and one report mentioned how many people chose the numbers 1, 2, 3, 4, 5, 6 in one draw: over 12000! Just having a winning number is no guarantee of riches, and picking numbers likely to be popular is going to reduce your potential gain.

Now suppose you buy 10 tickets – all with the same numbers. Does that improve your chances?

Obvious truths can hide traps for the unwary, and whilst the fallacies are pretty clear in the lottery examples, they are not always seen and understood in Sales Management.

Many studies have shown that call frequency works. One study looked at a large company's customer base, and asked the question: how many sales calls had it taken to persuade each customer to switch suppliers? The answers are in Table 4 below:

1 call	2%
2 calls	3%
3 calls	4%
4 calls	10%
5 or more	81%

Table 4: Conversion rate – number of calls to win the business

In other words, in over 80% of cases it took five or more calls.

Another result from a similar study showed that 88% of sales people gave up after three or less calls. The remaining 12% were responsible for 80% of sales. Clearly, number of calls, and number of calls per client, is a good predictor of sales success.

You will have guessed from the lead-in to this section that there is something wrong with this conclusion, and there is. The great danger of taking on board this obvious truth without deeper analysis is that sales management gets reduced to a numbers game, and, because computers are so good at numbers, often gets handed over to a computer to track and report on. What's wrong with counting sales calls and frequency? Two things, analogous to the fallacies around buying lottery tickets: first, not all sales are equal; and second, not all sales calls are equal.

When the emphasis is on call counting, sales people, being human, will typically respond by finding the easiest route to rack up the calls. This can mean calling on customers who are easy to visit, which is why every competitor's sales people are also calling on them. Readily accessible customers can mean customers with no loyalty: they will buy from you today, but in a month's time they have been visited by three other salespeople and have been persuaded to buy from someone else. Or they will share out their purchases over many suppliers, making for smaller deals with higher overheads.

A call is not a call is not a call. A way to rack up the calls is to ask politely just for two minutes and request a business card for proof of having visited: with a minimum of pushiness it becomes the quickest and easiest way for the prospect to get rid of you and you soon have a fistful of cards. A friendly customer who does steady, low-level business is another source of easy calls: the most dynamic and aggressive businesses haven't got time to spend on chit-chat. Junior people with no major decision-making powers like feeling important and will often more readily make themselves available than the real decision-makers.

To throw a little more confusion into the mix, there is a school of thought that says if you don't make a sale after three calls, cut your losses and move on. Oddly enough, there is empirical data to justify this approach, but as with all statistics you need to understand the hidden assumptions. If your calls are indeed all the same kind of calls, i.e. hard sales calls, then this is a fair rule of thumb. If you've tried three times and got nowhere, then trying still more times will likely not be much more successful. As the saying goes, if you keep doing what you have always done you will keep getting what you have always got.

The key to this apparent contradiction is that the successful sales person will keep making calls, not with the narrow aim of making a sale, but as part of the process of building the relationship. If you have targeted your customer as you should have, you are chasing a big prize. If you carefully cultivate the customer and build up the relationship – which may well take many more than three calls or contacts – then you can expect to reap the rewards.

Counting calls is enticing: CRM software is typically very good at this, makes it very easy, and has the allure of being an objective, quantifiable measure. Unfortunately, in many cases what it is measuring is as meaningful as counting how many lottery tickets you have bought without understanding their worth and the potential win you could get.

In this chapter we are going to talk about how to plan your calls and how to make each call count, rather than counting each call.

Proactive Targeting

Proactive targeting means identifying the customers you want to have as specifically as possible based on your Focus Factors, then going after them, allocating your time and resources appropriately based on their Gold, Silver or Bronze ranking. We have discussed this at length in Chapter 4 and here need only to refer you back to that chapter.

Activity Consistency

Let's look again at Table 4 on page 68. Why do repeated contacts work? Why don't 98% of customers sign the order on the first call? Why, in 80% of cases, does it take five or more calls before the deal is closed?

People buy from people, and they buy from people they trust. It's very rare to establish trust and a rapport in one contact, but over five or more you can build a relationship, prove your reliability, show tenacity, and show you are interested in your customer, his life, and his business. Can it be done in fewer contacts? Experience says not. 80% of the business needed five or more contacts, and the 12% of the sales team who did not give up after three calls closed 80% of the business.

It's very trendy to talk about Internet time, the accelerating pace of business, and trot out phrases like "you snooze you lose", but for all the changes in the business world it still takes time and repetition to build a solid relationship. It's certainly true that with modern technology it is possible to squeeze more customer contacts into a month than before. With email, SMS, and mobile phones added to telephones, post and face-to-face visits a relationship can progress faster, but it's by reducing the time between contacts, not the number of contacts.

The other lesson to learn from Table 4 is this: twenty calls spread over twenty customers have a 40% chance (20 x 2%) of winning one deal (for the mathematically purist, it actually works out to about 33%, but we needn't dig into statistics theory). Twenty calls spread over 5 customers give you a 57% chance of winning one deal. Twenty calls shared between two customers give you a near certainty of one deal and a better than even chance of getting two deals.

One of the authors of this book spent 18 months on a prospective customer before signing a contract that is still going strong 4 years later. It's a case study that illustrates the value of persistent, consistent selling:

Case study

The company was identified as an excellent prospect for training in the principles of Customer Quality Management, so the Regional Sales Manager was approached. He said No, not interested.

A bit of sleuthing with a secretary identified who the ultimate decision maker was, along with the warning that the company already had a specialist training company with a ten-year-long relationship.

The next step was to buy a bottle of wine with an unusual label – an individually numbered bottle – and deliver it to the decision maker's secretary with a card saying "Every day we do the impossible. Miracles take a little longer." The card was signed but with no contact information. Naturally, it stirred interest and curiosity.

Two weeks later, a phone call was made requesting an appointment, which was granted. Then followed 16 months of numerous contacts, birthday cards, postcards, messages and phone calls, which built up a relationship with many other people in the organisation along the way, as well as identifying the business influencers. Interestingly, towards the end of the period there was a management change, which was a setback, but the groundwork put in had spilled over to enough other people in the organisation that the management change proved to be no more than a hiccup. The relationship was rapidly re-built with the new manager, and a deal was closed not long afterwards.

A common mistake is to rush into the relationship. Do not try to move too fast: you need to be properly informed and hence prepared for the level of contact you are making. If after one or two contacts with the customer organisation you get an opportunity to pitch to the board, you should *not* grab it with both hands unless you are extraordinarily fortunate in gathering all the information you need in very short order. If you get it wrong, you will very seldom get a second chance: the higher up in the hierarchy you go, the less time your contacts are generally willing to afford you and the less tolerant they will be of mistakes.

A full-on pitch to the board needs careful preparation based on a thorough understanding of the customer's needs: go in too soon and you are signalling that you are out to close a deal for *your* benefit, not the customer's. Show respect for your customer by ensuring you know enough to be able to add value to the customer through your offering.

Your first meeting must be all eyes and ears. Use your mouth to clarify and solicit more information, not to sell. Get permission to talk to others in the organisation, learn and analyse, then you will be in a position to give a customised presentation that addresses the customer's needs and which the people in the organisation can relate to, and you will be prepared for objections.

Smoothing out the roller-coaster

Activity consistency is important not only in getting the sales, but also in controlling their timing. Most Sales Managers will be familiar with the classic sales roller coaster: it's either boom or bust. Sales are pouring in, or you're scrabbling for business.

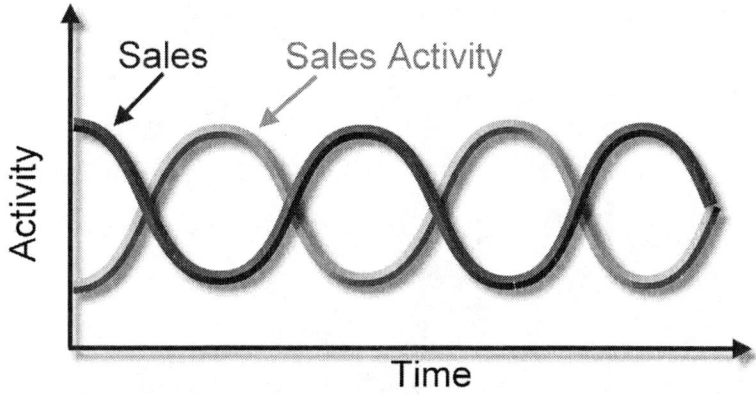

Figure 5: The Sales/Sales Activity Cycle

The problem is that when sales are good, the sales team get pats on the back. They are being rewarded not for what they are doing now, but for what they were doing some weeks or months ago. Sales activity tends to slacken off, and in a while sales start dropping. Panic sets in, triggering lots of selling activity – but at this stage, the sales team are being pressured for not bringing in the sales.

The sales roller-coaster makes it difficult to plan and run the business efficiently, but worse than that is that the contra-cycle of sales and sales activity reduces the effectiveness of the sales team. Sales lag sales activity by a significant amount, yet usually the sales team are recognised and rewarded based on sales. As a result, the pattern of reward and punishment is out of synch with what the sales team are actually doing, and can even be in direct opposition: praising and rewarding them when they are slacking off in the glow of a great month or quarter, berating them when they are frantically busy trying to generate new business.

This roller-coaster and counter-productive reward/punishment cycle arises when sales managers manage the sales instead of the sales process. Sales teams need to be measured and rewarded according to their customer-facing activity measured along three axes:

1.   The frequency of contact, qualified by:

2.   The quality of the contacts and

3.   The quality of the customers

If your sales team are maintaining frequency of contact with the right customers, and making the right kind of contact, the sales will follow.

The examples given of making contact with your customers in an interesting and different way (Valentine's cards, Lottery tickets) are ones that will work generically for most customers, but for the greatest effect you need to tailor your approach to each customer as an individual. To do that successfully you have to know your customer.

 **Myth 9: Selling is about talking business.**

If you only ever talk to your customers about business you will never gain insight into their personal interests, likes and dislikes, and so you will never be able to make your relationship go any deeper than pure business. Experience over many years of training in the field of CQM teaches that everyone readily acknowledges that business is about relationships, but very few take the steps to develop those relationships. Mixing in a reasonable amount of non-business time for topics like birthday wishes, congratulations on a child's achievement, congratulations or commiserations on the customer's favourite team's performance, or something related to a hobby or special interest, adds value to the relationship. Adding value to relationships shortens sales cycles and makes it far more likely that your customer will want to do business with you.

Chapter Summary – Building Relationships in a CQM Environment

You need a high frequency of contact with your customers to be able to build relationships, but this does not only mean physical sales calls. In fact, it is important to find many and varied ways of contacting your customers and to do so on both the business and personal levels.

The contact frequency and effort need to be in line with the sales potential of the customer, i.e. Gold, Silver or Bronze.

Activity consistency is vital to build long lasting relationships, as well as to smooth out the boom and bust sales roller coaster. Sales management needs to focus on the process, not the sales, because there is a lag between sales-building work and the sales. If only sales are rewarded, the sales team are being rewarded or censured out-of-phase with the selling efforts they are putting in.

Being different and interesting and making quality calls is far more important than making lots of calls.

6

Combining Frequency and Value-Add

Getting commitment from a customer is the outcome of a continuing process of many contacts with the customer that add value to him or her, in both business and personal spheres. In the course of those contacts, you will perform needs analyses and provide information, and as the relationship develops you will gather information, be granted permission and finally get customer commitment.

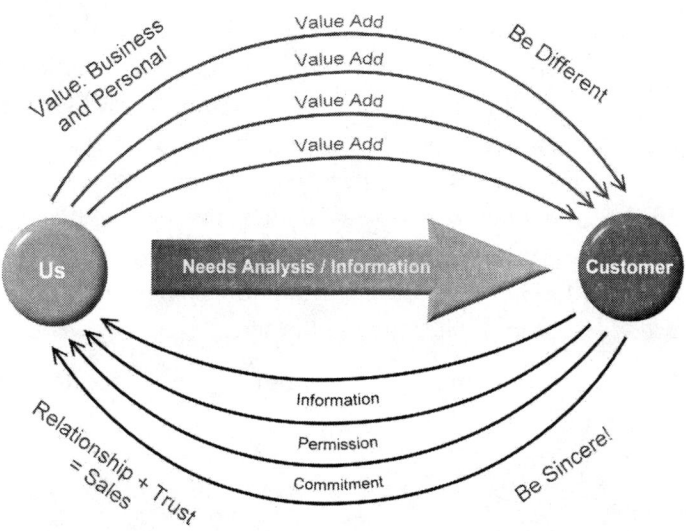

Figure 6: The Commitment Model

By "granted permission" we mean being allowed to gather further information and to see the customer more often. This is rarely if ever an explicit permission, of course: it's a permission that manifests as a willingness to answer questions, the volunteering of information, accepting your calls, and being available when meetings are requested.

Here's a little case study that illustrates the effectiveness of gaining customer commitment:

Case study

A pharmaceutical company had a chemotherapy product typically used in the treatment of lung cancer. The drug had been in the market 6 years, had a 35% market share, and was considered to be approaching end of life. As part of the process of implementing Customer Quality Management the sales manager cut the number of customers proactively targeted by 50%, from approximately 30 in each of chemotherapy and radiation therapy specialisations.

The reduction in customer database was accompanied by changing the frequency of contact. Previously, all customers were contacted once a quarter. A program of Call Quality Management set a target of "touching" each customer 52 times a year. These touches ranged across phone calls, emails, sending cuttings of interesting developments, 'chance' meetings in the car park or shopping centre, birthday or anniversary congratulations, house warming presents, hobby-related small gifts, and so on.

Over the next 6 months, the product market share more than doubled, to 75%.

 **Myth 10: Sales people use all the available resources and tools to make contact with customers.**

Most sales people who have not been trained and coached appropriately believe that selling is about making face-to-face sales calls, or using the telephone.

In the following pages we will look at how to make the right kind of contacts with customers in many different ways and how to gain their commitment.

Add Value!

The Yin and Yang of Sales

We are not going to drift off into Zen and eastern philosophy but we are going to delve into the duality of people's lives. Everyone in business also has a personal life; business still boils down to people doing business with people; so good selling means building relationships with your prospects and clients that add value to both their business and their personal lives.

> Examples of value-add contacts used by a medical representative:
> - Take a jug of refreshment for the waiting-room patients
> - Be able to work the switchboard so you can stand in for the receptionist and give her a 10-minute break
> - Give nurses practical advice on administering your products

We've discussed the danger of reducing sales management to call counting. Number and frequency of calls are undeniably indicators of sales but only as much as, say, the number and frequency of meals are indicators of good nutrition. The real challenge of sales (and management of sales) is to achieve balance and variety. An "A" customer may warrant weekly contact, but if you phone your customer once a week you risk becoming as welcome as fishcakes and chips served every day. On the other hand, if in the course of a month you visit once, pass on news of a competitor's press announcement once, send a reminder of the customer's wedding anniversary the day before, with a note of congratulations, and send a copy of an interesting article about Koi fish (you did know that was your customer's hobby, didn't you?), then you have made four contacts, each adding value to your customer in different ways.

There are many ways to make contact with your customers, as some of these examples show. Broadly, they can be classified as business or personal, direct or indirect. The classic sales call is business and direct: business-oriented and face-to-face. These are essential calls but not the stuff of which a healthy relationship is built. They are the bricks in a building, but you need mortar, doors, windows, paint, lights, carpets, even decorations, before you have a complete structure. Sales calls are also the most resource-intensive. Calling on a customer twice a month to discuss business will take up more of your selling time than one call plus the other activities in our examples, but which do you think will build the better relationship?

Here's a real-world example: an account manager working for a large financial services firm had been talking to a potential high-value client for months, receiving polite attention but no business. He learnt that his client was going on a cruise with his wife to celebrate their 40-year anniversary, so he arranged for flowers to be delivered on the day, with a fax of congratulations, by the captain of the ship to the couple's cabin. A few weeks later he was invited to meet with the client, heard that no-one else – not even family – had made the effort to mark the day, and left with a deal to manage R200m worth of assets.

In the context of making contact with customers, balance is the key. There should be a balance between business and personal, because you need to build relationships with the whole person. Don't confine your contacts to being strictly business-related, nor, for obvious reasons, go the other way. Also there must be a balance between direct and indirect, because you only have so much time available, and indirect contacts take much less of your time. However, don't think that because it takes less time it is of less value. Sending a postcard to a client when you are on holiday takes five minutes, but the impact of letting him know you thought of him even when on holiday is disproportionately high. Sending a note of congratulations on hearing that his company has closed a large contract, or on a son's bar-mitzvah, is quick but shows you care.

Be sincere. Don't do it if you don't mean it. If you don't take a genuine interest in your client's business and his life and take the trouble to find out what is important to him, you will churn out rote actions that will seem as plastic as they are, and get lost in the clutter. If you really know your customer you will find ways to make contact that add value and that stand out from the clutter: be sincere, and be different. If the heading of this section had been "A Balanced Approach to Sales", it would have earned the yawn it deserved. If you have read this far, you were drawn in by something that looked as though it would be a little different.

Another example from life: A sales representative noted from a client company's registration number that it was almost 10 years old, so after first discreetly confirming the date of founding, she arrived on the day with a large home-baked cake with ten candles. No-one in the company had even realised the significance of the date. Guess who was the talk of the company for weeks afterwards.

One more caveat on achieving balance: when making contact with your customers in the personal sphere, don't mix business talk in unless the customer invites it. If you meet a customer at the shopping centre, you are intruding into their private lives. When you are out shopping, or going to see a film, or on your way to a family meal, a pleasant brief encounter with an acquaintance is one thing, being buttonholed for business is quite another.

Building a relationship and trust between you and your customer changes the dynamics completely. The usual sales approach is one of trying to sell something to your customer. The goal is turn around the selling process so your customer is trying to buy from you.

Be interesting, be different

Consistent activity does not mean ringing the customer or prospect once a week and making the same old small talk, or worse, sales talk, every time. If you do, you will rapidly become a nuisance, but if you can bring something to the contact each time, you will become a friend. That something can be a smile, a chocolate, a piece of business information, a birthday or anniversary wish, a lead for your customer, a suggestion for someone who can solve a problem for them that you can't solve, a tip for her hobby, or anything else that will add a little something to his or her business or personal life.

Here are some examples:

- An office stationery company launched a three-day campaign aimed at their top customers leading up to Valentine's Day. The first day they delivered a card with a heart on it and the words "Somebody loves you". On day two, the heart on the card was opening and a small section of the supplier's logo showed behind, and the words read "Somebody still loves you". On day three, the heart was fully open and the supplier's logo was exposed, with the words "Company XXXX still loves you!"

- On St Patrick's Day, sales people dressed in green (for luck) and delivered lottery tickets to their customers. In preparation, customers were asked to choose their own numbers, and then the sales reps delivered the tickets. This kind of contact has a life: for a few days there is the anticipation of the result of the draw, and on the day of the draw the sales rep is brought to mind again. This is a self-generating contact!

Say what you will about the number of special days – most of them the inventions of the greeting card companies and florists – but they do present many excuses for making contact with your client with a little imagination and, usually, humour. Secretaries' Day, Bosses' Day, Burns Day, Left-handed Day, Mother's Day, Father's Day... search the Internet and have fun!

Getting the Mix Right

In this chapter and the next, we devote a lot of attention to building up the personal side of relationships with your customers. The reason we put so much emphasis on this is because it is the side that is so often neglected, but you mustn't lose sight of the fact that the bulk of the interactions with your customers will, and should, be business-oriented. A good rule of thumb is that around 30%, or a quarter to a third, of your company's contacts with your customers should have a personal angle.

Business Influencers – Matching Strategies to People

Unless you are dealing with retail sales or one-man bands, your client companies are not monolithic entities: they are collections of individuals. A doctor's practice, for example, is not just the doctor: it is typically the doctor, a receptionist, a nurse and a bookkeeper, and some of them may not be immediately obvious to you. The bookkeeper for example may only be there part-time, but could still be an influencer that you need to take cognisance of. You need to plan your strategies with each customer around the individuals involved and to understand the rôle that each plays.

When you have the basic information you can then categorise your contacts in the client organisation into Gold, Silver and Bronze levels within that organisation so you can devote appropriate shares of your limited resources to the individuals involved. Review what we said about Business Influencers in the previous chapter: people with no direct buying decision-making power can nonetheless have a huge influence on whether you get the order. It could be the secretary who decides to let your call through, the technical person who says yea or nay on compatibility, integration or suitability issues, the Human Resources person who comments on the impact it will have on staffing, or any of many others that you might not have considered.

When you have identified your key influencers, do something special for them. You need to be creative in your approach, and obtain information on their goals, objectives, likes, dislikes and interests, on both the business and personal levels. Make whatever you do different, special or personal, so your Gold customers know they are being treated like Gold!

Here are some ideas on how to approach the different kinds of Business Influencers:

The Guide: This is the person that will give you all the background information you need and guide you to success.

Typical Personality: A Supporter. The relationship and trust are important to them. Do not push them too quickly: the Guide needs to feel comfortable with you before starting to divulge information.

Goal: To build a personal, high-trust relationship.

Invite your Guide for meetings outside of the normal business environment, possibly for coffee or breakfast. People can talk more freely when not in front of their peers.

Find three or four ways to add value to the Guide in his or her personal capacity. *Listen* to learn what makes him or her tick.

Have regular meetings to understand the business better, to learn the business focus, and find out what volume of business they could potentially give you.

Find out who the other business influencers are, and who their current suppliers are.

Introduce your guide to appropriate management in your organisation.

The Veto Power: This person wields ultimate power over the deal, and may well not be the person who signs the contract.

Typical Personality: A Driver. Focus on the business side of the relationship first and only later can you start to build a personal relationship. They do not like details and chit-chat – get to the point quickly.

Goal: To develop a high level relationship between this person and your senior management. Make sure this person understands the value you bring to his or her organisation.

Put your emphasis on facilitating value-adding contacts (not just meetings for meetings' sake) between the Veto Power and different members of your management, typically once a quarter. Plan the meetings well in advance and have objectives in mind: ask yourself how the meeting will add value to the Veto Power's life.

Hold regular meetings to discuss the value of your company's products or services to your client's business, and how you could improve what you offer. You need to understand the client's business well before you can do this.

Email, fax or deliver news about his or her industry, as well as items of interest on a personal level.

Take the Veto Power to an event or VIP function at least once a year.

The Affected: The Affected are the people that will be directly affected by the products or services you offer.

Typical Personality: An Expressive. They are outspoken and say what they feel. They need to feel important and to be kept informed. Compliment them regularly but sincerely.

Goal: These people are your eyes and ears on the ground who will be able to tell you directly how your offerings are working (or not) for them. You want to build your relationships with the leaders in this group to the point where they will contact you first with good news or bad about your product or service.

If you achieve your goal, you will know about any hitch before the Veto Power gets to hear of it. They will also ensure that positive news gets relayed either to you or to the Veto Power – and if it's to you, make sure you pass it on!

Pop in regularly to see how they are, and remember to include both business and personal aspects.

Take them a cool drink on a hot day, remember birthdays and anniversaries. News of your thoughtfulness will spread.

Be proactive in informing or reminding them about upcoming service or product changes or new releases.

The Gatekeeper: Gatekeepers are there to protect their companies or managers.

Typical Personality: An Analytical type. They focus on the details of a product or service. Take time to give them all the information, and try to create new ways to present your information in a statistical or graphical format. It is important for them to know that there is no risk involved in doing business with you.

Goal: Give them enough information for them to trust you, your company and the products or services you offer.

Gatekeepers can be as varied as the receptionist or the Financial Manager. The Gatekeepers need to know that you and your company can be trusted: focus on building trust and supply ample information about your company, products and services.

Send statistics on what they have purchased from you and the benefits they have enjoyed through doing business with you.

Fax or email interesting bits of news relevant to their business as well as to their personal interests or hobbies.

The Curve Ball: Curve Balls come from unexpected quarters (which is why we call them Curve Balls). Anyone or anything that can influence your business is your business, and you need to be on the lookout for them. It could be a client who had a bad experience with you who puts off an existing or potential client, or someone with a personal grudge against you or someone in your organisation, or be a bad product review in a magazine, or any of dozens of other possibilities.

When you spot a Curve Ball, put a plan together to handle the negative influence. Be humble and use your relationships and company resources to deal with it. Business studies are littered with examples of companies dealing with Curve Balls with arrogance and denial, and paying the price. Far rarer are the shining examples like Johnson and Johnson when they had to deal with cyanide-laced Tylenol: it took time, but they emerged stronger and with an enhanced reputation because they acted decisively and with humility to deal with the problem.

Dealing with Business Influencers is not just the responsibility of the sales person, it extends upwards to the first-line manager and senior management, and across to the other departments.

First-line sales managers should be involved with Gold and Silver clients on a regular basis:

- Attend at least one function per quarter with the sales person to meet Business Influencers.

- Proactively call the Guide to thank him or her for the support.

- Attend at least one breakfast or coffee session per quarter with the Gold clients.

- Make sure the National Sales Manager is involved in at least some of these meetings, and is kept up to date with the Gold clients and the contact people in those clients.

- When your Gold clients are bedded down, start spreading the process to Silver clients.

Senior management must be involved with Gold clients.

- Make contact with them. For example, write a letter thanking them for their business or inviting them to do (more) business with you.

- Make sure the identities, importance and status of Gold

customers is communicated to everyone in the company.

- Give recognition to staff who have gone the extra mile.

- Get Marketing to devise customised activities for Gold clients.

- Get everyone involved in gathering information and relaying news about Gold clients to the sales person involved.

Company resources such as Accounts, Logistics and Technical Services need to be involved.

- Where they can add value, invite them to meetings with the customer. Remember that giving your support team more insight into the customers and their needs adds value to both sides, as the support team get more job satisfaction by seeing the positive effect they can have, and the customers get better service.

- Administrative staff can take on some of the more routine contacts, such as calling or emailing clients on their birthdays, on behalf of the sales person or on their own account.

Chapter Summary – Combining Frequency and Value-Add

Your goal as a business is to get commitment from the client, which you will get by gathering information, gaining trust and being "granted permission", and finally establishing a sound relationship.

To achieve this you have to add some value to the client's life every time you make contact. You need to treat your clients as whole people, and find ways to add value to both their business and personal lives.

Your activities have to be matched to your Business Influencers – the people in the client organisation who have different levels and forms of control over the business that will come your way.

Selling is not the task of the sales team alone: other levels and departments in the organisation must be involved, especially with your Gold customers.

Know Your Customer

The submarine commander's dilemma

Not knowing your customers faces you with the submarine commander's dilemma. If a submarine commander comes across a convoy he can only see one or two ships at a time. As soon as he fires his torpedoes the escorting destroyers will be after him, so he has to make a call on which ship to target. If he has no idea what ships are in the convoy, he won't know which ship is the richest prize.

A sales person with insufficient knowledge of the customers is in a similar predicament: with limited information, you don't know what is the best target for your limited resources (time and budget). Spending them on the wrong customer leaves you like the commander who has fired his torpedoes at the little freighter when the massive cargo ship is out of sight.

Getting away from WIIFM

WIIFM stands for "What's In It For Me?", and unfortunately it's what drives most salespeople. Naturally the underlying motive for salespeople is indeed their personal benefit, but if it is the primary motivator then it will be self-destructive. Your customers are not interested in making *your* life better, and if they once sense that that is all you are interested in, they will rapidly lose interest in you. It's a sad, brutal truth, but you have to accept it! The salesperson's task is to add value to the customer's life in as many ways as possible, and to do that you need information.

Here's a simple exercise we use in training sessions. The students are told, "Add value to me." The discussion follows roughly these lines:

Class: How?

Trainer: Well, you could wish me happy birthday on my birthday.

Class: But when is your birthday?

It's obvious, isn't it? If you don't know anything about your customer or your customer's business, you are not going to be able to add value to his personal or business life. If you go into a sales situation with your sole focus being to sell your product or service you are starting with a serious handicap. You are expecting your customer to see how he will benefit from doing business with you, or worse, you may only be thinking about how you will benefit from doing business with your customer!

Consider this example of an insurance salesman – let's call him Gerald – who tried to build on a chance meeting with an acquaintance at a coffee shop. Gerald bumped into his acquaintance by chance, and asked if he could sit with him for breakfast. A few minutes in, Gerald said: "I've got a great new life insurance product which guarantees acceptance without a medical. Are you interested?" Gerald's prospect knew that he was more than adequately insured, and in good health, so the thoughts that went through his mind were "How can he offer me that without even asking if I needed insurance?", "Does he think I look ill?", and "He's just trying to sell me whatever he has, he doesn't care what I need." In thirty seconds, Gerald destroyed any chance of ever doing business with his acquaintance.

In another case, a company submitted a 250-page proposal for a contract, but did not get the deal. They asked one of the authors for an assessment of why the proposal might have failed. The answer was clear: in 250 pages, the proposal covered at length what they had to offer, who they were, and their qualifications and experience. Not one paragraph showed any evidence of having researched the customer or the customer's needs or possible solutions.

Knowing your customer is so important that your first contact with a prospective customer should be focused on gathering information to understand how you can add value.

Gathering Information

If a customer says: "I can't make next Thursday, it's my wedding anniversary", you can say "Oh, well how about Friday?", or you can say "Really? How many years is it? Congratulations!" and note it and record it. Gather all the information you can about your customers: marital status, children, birthdays of the whole family, choice in reading, films and TV, teams supported, interests, religion (what are the special days?), where they live. If the relationship is close enough, you can delve deeper into what his or her goals are in life and what New Year's resolutions have been made.

Business information is generally easier to get. Most obviously, you can always ask your customer to tell you about their business, and most companies will have a web site that you can study. Customers are usually more than happy to tell you about their business, obviously stopping short of disclosing sensitive information. Start your relationship by listening: a first call on a prospective customer should begin with open-ended enquiries, like the following:

- I don't want to sell you anything until I know what you need. Tell me about your business.
- What is your business vision? How do you aim to get there?

- Who are your customers?

- What do you see as your most important requirements from a supplier?

- Who are your current suppliers? Are you happy with their service?

With an established customer, you can explore your company's relationship with the customer:

- Are you happy with our product/service? What changes would you like?

- What can we do to improve?

You should be aware of events happening in and around your Gold and Silver client companies, and asking questions that flow from them:

- Will the restructuring/merger/acquisition affect the decision-making process? Whose positions are going to change?

- When Mr. A leaves, who will be replacing him? Can I arrange to meet his replacement?

- Will Company Y's new product/advertising campaign/strategy affect your business?

There are many outside sources you can tap as well: Internet, friends, secretaries, other companies you deal with, newspapers, the trade press. When you know something about the business, you can do some research on the business' market place and get some ideas of who the competition is, what factors are influencing their market, what opportunities they have, and what problems they may be facing.

Practical examples

Having the information is the first step, now you have to use it.

The perennial obstacle to putting "Know your customer" into practice is that people don't know how, so we will give a few more examples and some suggestions on how to generate more ideas.

1) A salesperson in office stationery had been doing steady but unexciting business with a customer for 6 years. Following training on the principle of CQM, she decided to try to build rapport through knowing something about her customer's personal life. She discovered from a chance remark that he was a keen camper, of the kind who goes into trackless areas with 4x4 vehicles, which happened to be her passion. The call then turned into 45 minutes of swapping tales and information, and from then on they continued to exchange tips and news in between doing business – the level of which grew many fold over the following months.

2) A pharmacist was renowned for being the difficult customer in town, dreaded by all the sales reps. One sales rep, though, picked up that he was a soccer fan who supported Arsenal, so he researched the club and next time he called on the pharmacist remarked: "I believe you're an Arsenal supporter? I can see why: I've read they haven't lost a game in 43 matches!" The pharmacist's face lit up as he launched into an animated discussion of what made Arsenal such a good team. From then on the sales rep was always – and solely – greeted with a smile whenever he called.

3) An account manager was struggling to get business from a prospect. They got on well enough person-to-person, but the customer said as a matter of policy he wanted to give the business to people of his own culture. The account manager picked up that the customer and his wife had a habit of going out once a week to a particular restaurant followed by a show, so he told his wife that they were about to start the same practice. The two couples met 'by

chance' at the restaurant then bumped into each other again at the show. The same thing happened the next week, and soon they were sharing a table. A few months later, the prospect became a customer.

4) A salesman heard and recorded a customer's chance comment that her husband was mad about cars, and would love to experience driving a Porsche Boxster. He made an appointment to see her on what he knew to be the day before her wedding anniversary, and asked what she'd arranged for the day. She hadn't done anything special. He then presented her with a file of collected information on Boxster history and facts, and while they were talking the local Porsche dealer phoned (by arrangement) to arrange a test drive for her husband. Not only did he cement a relationship with the customer, the rest of the company got to hear of it and he got the reputation of being someone who took a real interest in his customers.

5) A sales person on a country trip passed through a small town well-known as a trout fisherman's favourite haunt. Recalling that one of his most important customers was a keen trout fisherman, he stopped in at one of the specialty stores and asked for their recommendations for flies that were well-suited to the area and the time of year and bought a selection. On his return to base he called his customer and made an appointment to see him, and when they met he presented him with the flies and explained how he was passing through the area and thought of him and his passion for catching trout. The customer was both impressed and appreciative.

The points to be taken from these examples are first, that information is constantly flowing past and usually being ignored. In the first example, the sales lady must in six years have heard mention many times of clues that her customer was interested in camping, but she was so focused on business that she did not pick up and act on the information.

Second, everyone has hot buttons. There is always something that someone has an interest in, and if you make the effort to share in it in some way, you will get the appreciation.

Third, you can manufacture coincidences, as long as you don't misuse them. If the account manager in the third example had used the dinner-table to discuss business, it would not have worked (unless the customer initiates it, but even then be careful not to bore the spouse).

Chapter Summary – Know Your Customer

You can only add value to a customer if you know him or her well, from both business and personal perspectives. You need a continuing exercise of gathering and updating information about your customers, and looking for ways to build on that knowledge.

Good information opens up opportunities for positive ways to touch your customer's life: use the information to increase contact frequency and activity consistency.

Be sincere!

8

Putting it into Practice

The underlying concepts behind Customer Quality Management are not particularly difficult to grasp, but as always with a change in strategy the challenge comes in the implementation. And, also as always with a change in strategic approach, implementation will not be successful without buy-in from the top.

The absolute, non-negotiable base requirement is that senior management must be behind the shift from conventional CRM to CQM. They must understand the need to focus on the sales process that will fill the pipeline instead of on this month's sales figures; they must be using the principles of CQM to secure the future rather than applying conventional CRM to study the present. No amount of pressure from the top will grow the current month's sales by 40%: it's already too late for that. On the other hand, focussing on the process can grow business by 30% or 40% or 50% in three or six months' time.

Before we delve into implementation details, we'll look at an example of CQM being put into practice with the full backing of senior management.

Case study

A logistics company, which we'll call GSB Logistics, adopted the principles of CQM and set about categorising their customers. They identified many customers who did not even manage Bronze status. Generally these were the smaller companies, but not always: the important criterion was what value they represented to GSB Logistics. The next step was the leap of faith that would not have been possible without the support of senior management: once GSB Logistics had identified the low-value customers they called them to explain why GSB Logistics did not think they could offer them the appropriate service at a cost-effective price. This first step was expected to create considerable unhappiness in the customer base, but in fact was relatively painless. Most companies appreciate, even if not consciously, that they are better served by a service provider to whom they are important. GSB Logistics was also at pains to assist those customers make an orderly transition to alternative service providers.

At the other end of the scale, GSB Logistics had identified a Gold prospect that they wanted to target. The sales representative started to build a relationship with the decision-maker over many weeks. The key selling proposition was that GSB Logistics was the quality, solid and reliable service provider, drawing the analogy of a Mercedes Benz truck rather than a nondescript little pick-up. The client got to the point of saying he wanted to give GSB Logistics the business but he was locked into his current logistics contract for another ten months.

A few days later the sales rep visited the client with a beautiful Mercedes Benz model kit, saying he would have time to build it while the current contract ran out. Two weeks later, she received a call from the client saying he had found a way out of his current contract and GSB Logistics could get the business immediately.

GSB Logistics' sales rep had built the relationship to the point where the customer wanted to give her the business. The model kit had been intended to serve as a long-term memory jogger, as well as a light-hearted way of emphasising GSB Logistics' value proposition. It turned out to be a catalyst to closing the business even sooner than hoped.

The Four Pillar Business Plan

The principles discussed in the preceding chapters can be embodied in a four pillar business plan:

Identify the right clients. Classify your clients – potential and actual – as Gold, Silver and Bronze. See Chapter 4, *Focus Factors,* p. 43.

Develop customised strategies. Formulate strategies for each class of client and their stage of development, i.e. Attract, Expand or Sustain. See Chapter 4, *The Second Dimension,* p. 54

Set contact schedule targets. Determine targets for both frequency and kind of contacts appropriate to each strategy. See Chapters 5 and 6.

Identify ways to add value. Look for ways to add value to your customers' lives, both business and personal. Remember that your goal is to build relationships, because people do business with people. See Chapters 6 and 7.

Underpinning the four pillars are three base requirements:

Know your customer. If you don't know your customer, you can't add value. See Chapter 7.

Discretion. Sales people need to exercise some discretion, and sales managers need to give them that discretion. Your business will depend on the relationship your sales people have with their customers, and no one-size-fits-all approach can take account of the complexities and potential richness of interpersonal relationships. Sales people should have their own budgets and the freedom to allocate them as they see fit, with support and guidance from their first-line managers. There will of course generally be overriding company policies: for example, your business may decree that entertaining clients at strip clubs is not permitted.

Execute your plan. It's not enough to have a plan. Many plans are drawn up and then lost in a drawer or buried under other papers on a desk. Once you have a plan, execute it!

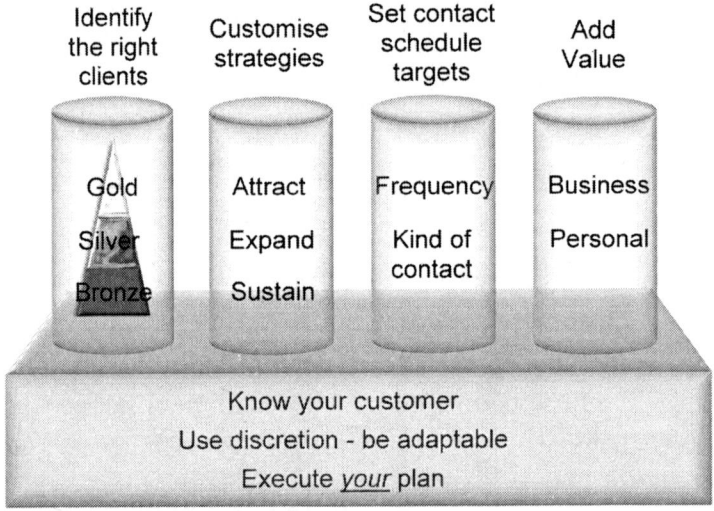

Figure 7: The Four-Pillar Business Plan

The implementation of the business plan requires the involvement of everyone in the organisation, but there are different levels of criticality. A full implementation of CQM takes time, and there is cultural inertia to overcome. Given that you are not going to be able to address everyone in the organisation at the same time, you will need to prioritise your training and spreading of the word, so it's important to understand the different levels. Broadly, you can segment your people into four groups:

- **Resources**. Everyone is important, for the reasons we have covered at various places in this book, but your resource departments are not absolutely critical to implementation. It is critical to ensure that they do not indulge in negative actions that destroy your sales efforts, but positive support can follow later once you have your sales team on the right wavelength.

- **Senior management**. Senior management are not critical to implementation but they must support it in actions and words. They must share the language and buy in to the principles; and they must be committed to play their part, for example in visiting Gold customers. Because of the weight senior management carry in an organisation, negative comments or any indication that they don't really believe in the plan can instantly cripple it. Above all, senior management must be committed to measuring the process, not the outcome. They must accept and believe that if the process is right, the sales will follow. The moment they waver and start pushing for this month's sales figures the plan will start to unravel. The senior management team especially are like a rowing eight: if one or two are out of phase, they mess up the entire crew effort.

- **Sales team**. The sales team is obviously key to the success of CQM and it is essential that they get the principles conveyed to them in the purest form, not diluted, filtered or re-interpreted by management. In other words, they need to get trained by specialists who thoroughly understand CQM. These are the front-line people who will spearhead your business strategy, identify the Gold and Silver customers, and be the primary interface between your company and your customers. Your best option to grow your business significantly is to correctly target the customers with the greatest potential value so your sales team have to be very clear on how to find and develop that potential. The acid test for the sales team is to ask the question: how do you develop a Bronze customer into a Gold customer? If they answer with anything other than "you can't!" then they have not understood CQM. (See *The Second Dimension* on p. 54).

- **First-line management**. First-line management are the most critical group of all. They will be responsible for implementation of the strategy and coaching the sales team. They have to understand the value of the different customers and the distinction between quantity and quality of sales calls. They must understand too that there are many ways to touch customers apart from face-to-face visits and telephone calls, and that customers are whole people with both business and personal interests. They must keep the focus on the sales process, customer quality management and call quality management, and let the actual sales come out of the process. First-line management is crucial to the sustainability of a CQM strategy.

Management at all levels must understand that pressure for sales *this* month is pointless: it's already too late. The pressure must be on the process, to build the relationships that will fill the pipeline, typically three months ahead of actual orders. No matter how diligently you scour the cornfield, if you didn't plant enough seeds you will not gather more crops.

Figure 8: Building the Pipeline illustrates the difference between "old school" sales management and the CQM approach. The old school approach is focused on this month's sales, with management attention and pressure all on this goal.

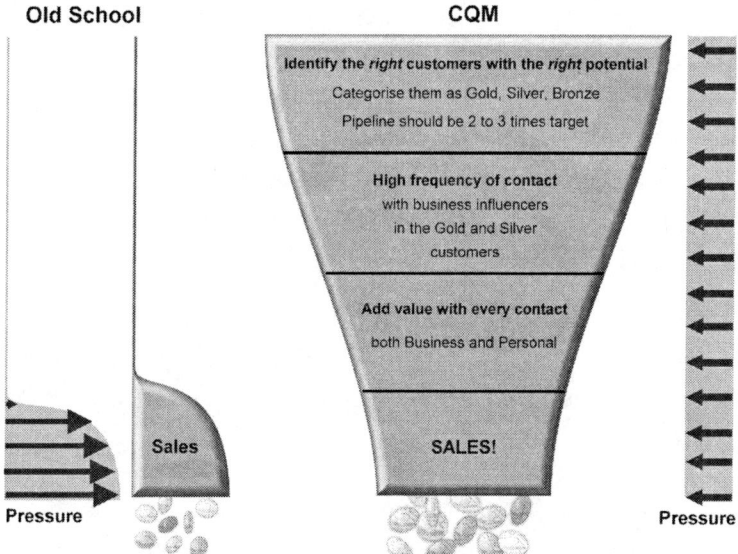

Figure 8: Building the Pipeline

When you invest in managing the quality of your customers and the quality of the contacts you have with them, you will build the relationships that will lead to sales. Your process becomes:

1. Identify and qualify your customers and prospects and build a potential sales pipeline of two to three times your sales target.

2. Design a contact frequency plan suited to your different customers and targeting the business influencers in those customer companies.

3. Make sure you add value with every contact and make sure you address both business and personal aspects.

The sales *will* follow!

The figure illustrates a "steady state" that you should reach after about four months, where management attention is evenly spread across the range of CQM activities. In the initial stages (two to three months) the pressure on the final stage, sales, should be reduced with full concentration on the first three stages. Your sales team will be going through a steep learning curve and will hit a trough where nothing seems to be working: this is the danger zone your sales team – and management – will go through as the organisation passes through the stages of change that we discuss later in this chapter (see p. 114, *Making It Happen*). At this stage, the process is all important, and worrying about short-term sales will seriously threaten the implementation of CQM.

The brief case histories that follow illustrate how CQM can fail or succeed in varying degrees according to how well the implementation is carried out.

> *Case study: how not to do it*
>
> A supplier of heavy goods vehicles embarked on a CQM strategy without getting buy-in from their overseas head office. The initial steps of introducing the sales team to the principles of CQM and identifying, through focus factors, their Gold customers were carried out. The sales people started strategic efforts to win business from Gold prospects, but then pressure came from the overseas senior management to meet month-end sales goals. Local management began interfering on the ground level, pushing the sales team to chase quick deals. The sales team spent so much time on trying to close quick wins that all long-term strategic actions were pushed into the background.
>
> In this case, CQM was killed by lack of buy-in from the top, and the company continued to operate in barely-in-time month-to-month survival mode.
>
> *Case study: successful implementation derailed*
>
> A chemical supply company successfully implemented CQM and saw sales growing dramatically. A year into the new approach, the decision was taken to introduce a CRM

system, supposedly to reinforce the strategy. Unfortunately the CRM system selected had two fatal shortcomings:

1. The primary performance metric produced was a simplistic count of sales calls.

2. The system ran on hand-held Personal Digital Assistants (PDAs) linked via the GSM network, which showed managers in real time every time a sales person logged on, and generated vast quantities of unfiltered information which was not sorted or qualified against the principles of CQM.

The consequences of these two shortcomings were that a regimen of micro-management set in, and the sales team became measured against the wrong metrics. You get results according to how you measure and recognise performance, and in this case they lost sight of call quality management and the CQM strategy, smothered in a welter of data about the wrong things. Sales started floundering, and the sales managers, overloaded with data but little information, were polishing the handrails on the Titanic: trying to fix little things whilst the basic strategy was being destroyed.

Case study: a good recovery

Senior management need to have a realistic expectation of how long it takes to see the fruits. A financial services company went through a CQM implementation with the right backing from management and for the first few weeks the managers and sales team had weekly meetings focused on the CQM process. Then, after a month had passed, senior management started asking where the sales were. A pointed enquiry from senior management gets sharper and more concentrated as it trickles down through the organisation, and very soon the sales people got into panic mode and started chasing short-term deals.

The consultant championing the implementation (the

change agent – discussed later under *Making It Happen* on p.114) saw what was happening and was able to get management to allow the process to run properly. The important point was not to get management to ease up, but to get them to have faith that if the pipeline was properly built, the sales would come, and hence put the pressure on ensuring the process was followed.

The results were everything they could have hoped for: from a base of $160m a month the value of deals after 4 months rose by $60m per month, and after 12 months were up by $140m per month – nearly double.

Case study: a home run

A merchant bank was chasing a deals target of $1.5m a month, but the total sales pipeline was only $1m. Clearly, there was no hope of making target. The bank decided to implement a CQM strategy and did it by the book. Within months they had boosted the sales pipeline to $3m by identifying and targeting their Gold and Silver customers and focusing on building relationships with them. In less than a year they were making target easily instead of falling short by 50% or more.

First Steps

Given that we have senior management backing, where do we start?

Explain the Strategy and Vision

Senior management should already have a strategic view of the company and understand the principles of alignment of business objectives, market opportunity and business resources discussed in Chapter 3: *The Three Pillars of Business* (p. 21), but the strategy and vision need to be explained to the people who will drive implementation of CQM. These will be Sales Managers, influential sales people, and heads of departments such as logistics and accounts.

Senior management should accept input from the people in the field and in the workplace, but need to keep decision-making at the appropriate level. Setting the core strategy is senior management's responsibility and should be done by senior management; explaining what that strategy is and selling it internally. This is where senior management gets together with first-line management and senior sales people.

There is a school of thought that says sales people don't need to included in discussions of company strategy 'because they won't understand it'. If your sales people don't understand your strategy, they will not be able to identify the customers with the real potential to add value to your business. It's the job of management to explain the strategy in terms and at a level that makes sense to the sales team, and indeed to everyone else in the organisation. Without it, you will possibly get by. With it, you will get the kind of business-changing results that are quoted in the final chapter of this book.

The sales leadership and the resource areas need a common understanding of how customers will be classified and targeted in the context of the company strategy. Sales people must start thinking about how to identify the Gold, Silver and Bronze customers (*Focus Factors*: p. 43) and to do so with input from the resource areas. If sales and support departments don't have a shared understanding of what makes a good customer then internal conflict will arise. If, for example, the technical support team think a particular customer is unreasonably demanding and is being cultivated by a sales person just with an eye on commission, that customer will not get the best treatment. They may think that the customer will generate large sales but at a very high cost in support. They may be right, but if the customer is strategic to the business, and the support team understand that, then they will still provide the support. If they don't understand the strategic value, they will feel that they are doing all the hard work for the selfish interests of one sales person, and may even deliberately sabotage deals.

Explaining the strategy and vision is a starting point, but also something that will need to be done repeatedly. The management need to understand that what seems clear to them because it is their primary focus and continually top of mind for them, will seem briefly clear to people with other day-to-day responsibilities, then fade and become vague and confused.

Develop Focus Factors and Contact Frequency Plans

After initial presentation of a high-level view of the strategy to key influencers (sales management, senior sales people, heads of departments) move on to defining the focus factors.

The first phase is with management who, building on the three pillars of Chapter 3, will identify the market(s) to be focused on.

The second phase is to bring in relevant sales and line management to identify focus factors in each market. These focus factors will define the ideal customers: those who have the most potential to help the business achieve its goals, whether those goals are turnover, profit, brand building, market share, or whatever other objectives the business has set.

Targets must be set for frequency of contact with reference to the customer assessment grid (see Figure 3 on p. 55). The targets will of course differ for Gold, Silver and Bronze, and may differ for each of Attract, Expand, Sustain. If there are multiple markets being targeted, then differences between markets may also be appropriate.

Contact frequency planning is primarily the responsibility of the sales department, but support departments should have an awareness of the sales teams' targets and be included in their contact schedules. For example, contact from the accounts department to forestall credit limit problems; or from logistics to make special arrangements for deliveries to Gold customers; or from technical support to ensure smooth implementation of pilot projects; and so on.

Measurement and Reporting

If you can't measure it, it won't happen!

Everyone reacts to incentives and people's natural tendency is to follow the line of least resistance to achieve their personal goals. By the nature of sales people and how they are recompensed, this is most especially true of the sales team. If you don't incentivise the sales team in a way consistent with the business objectives, you will not get the results you want. The commonest errors in this regard are to incentivise sales people on sales when you actually want to maximise net profit, and to push for short term sales to make this month's targets at the expense of building the pipeline for the next few months, which at best gets you on the sales roller coaster (see p. 73, *Smoothing out the roller-coaster*).

To be able to align sales incentives with business goals, you must have a reporting system that measures the right things.

To implement CQM, you need a reporting system that tells you if your sales team are seeing the right clients, at the right frequency, with the right tools (visits, phone calls, emails, social encounters) (see Chapter 5: *Building Relationships in a CQM Environment*, p. 67). This could be anything from a paper-based system to a purpose-built CQM system such as Tracer (www.tracercqm.com).

CRM systems can provide some of the reporting needed, but be aware that most of them focus on call counting with little or no qualification of the quality of the call or of the customer.

A purpose-built CQM system will contextualise the calls within your Gold/Silver/Bronze ratings of the client companies and the contacts within those companies. It will provide an information gathering system that will make it easy for the sales people to capture business and personal information about their clients quickly while it is still fresh and before it is forgotten, and it will have a reminder system to mark important dates such as birthdays, religious festivals, major industry events, and events of particular interest to specific contacts. Nowadays the most obvious platform is a mobile handheld PDA or Pocket PC linked to a central database over cellular data links.

Reporting should also look forward. Sales people should develop a contact plan for the next two weeks, tied in with the contact frequency targets established earlier and related to the Gold/Silver/Bronze matrix, and then **be measured by the plan!** Only too often such plans are made then filed in a drawer and never referred to again: make a plan, then stick to it. Sales managers: measure your team by their adherence to their plans.

Structured Coaching from First-Line Managers

 Myth 11: First-line managers understand that their role is to coach and develop their sales people.

Many first-line managers see themselves as "the boss", or first among equals, and it's not uncommon for a top sales person to be promoted on the basis of their sales ability, not their coaching and development abilities (see the next myth below).

First-line managers must coach their sales team on strategy but must also understand what they do minute by minute. Guidelines are that they should spend about two hours per sales person per month discussing their strategy and coaching them, and spend one full day per month out in the field with each sales person. A full day tells the manager far more than two half days or scattered visits because it takes half a day for barriers to start breaking down, and also because it's hard for a sales person who is ill-prepared to cover up lack of preparation or poor customer knowledge for a full day.

The 80/20 principle is something we have referred to many times, but with sales teams there is typically a slightly different breakdown you should understand: the 10/80/10 principle.

 Myth 12: Top salespeople know what they do right

Even successful salespeople seldom know what they do to be successful. As with any other skill, being good at it does not mean you are able to teach it or analyse it.

10% of your sales team will be successful almost regardless of the environment they operate in, though with the right environment they will be that much more successful.

80% of them will succeed if you make it possible for them to succeed, with coaching and support from their managers, and from the rest of the organisation.

10% are not going to be successful, no matter what you do.

The primary task of the first-line manager is to get the best from the 80%. The top 10% will benefit as well, and he can mitigate the effects of the bottom 10%, but your real growth opportunities will flow from the 80%.

Making It Happen

The first step in implementing a new strategy is to write it down. Having a reference document helps you to keep focused on your strategy, and gives your strategy a years-long life. In all organisations people come and go: without a written reference document the strategy will get distorted, concepts will be passed on to newcomers incompletely and with changes, and people will forget why they did things they way they did. Keep in mind that implementing CQM requires effort: the rewards are great but they come at a price, and people will slip back into bad habits if you let them.

An implementation plan template can be downloaded from www.tracercqm.com/cqm.

One of the earliest requirements in a successful CQM strategy implementation is to identify a champion or change agent. People and organisations have an inherent resistance to change. Almost universally, we are more comfortable doing what we have always done rather than doing something differently. Your change agent will be someone who drives change and overcomes that resistance. It could be a consultant, or a newly-created position. It's seldom wise to select someone in an existing position and just add the change agent role to their job description: existing people are usually busy and have other priorities and your implementation plan will be pushed down the priority list.

If a new position is created it would usually be someone who reports to the National Sales Manager with a title like Sales Strategy Manager or Strategic Sales Manager. Key tasks for the Strategic Sales Manager would be (1) regular meetings with regional sales managers, keeping them on track; (2) field work to assess achievements and shortcomings first-hand from the front line; (3) coordinating between sales and support departments to achieve the alignment of resources behind business objectives and resolve cooperation issues.

Change takes time – instant results are not the norm. You should expect sales to stay stable or even drop a little for a month or two. As the sales team are exposed to the concepts, they will go through a four-stage process:

- Enthusiasm: Initial exposure to the concepts generates excitement because it all seems to straightforward, logical and full of promise. At this stage, they have not yet acquired the skills and do not realise what they don't know.

- Disillusion and demotivation: The initial enthusiasm is replaced by despondency as it seems so much harder to put it all into practice than at first thought. They are now conscious of their lack of skills. This low point typically comes in the first two weeks into the implementation.

- Recovery: As the skills are acquired they are putting them into practice and starting to see results. It is still tough going, but they are making progress; they have the skills but still have to work at applying them.

- Unconscious competence: The skills are now part of their everyday behaviour.

It's like learning to drive a car: at first it seems so easy and exciting, in a quiet back road, in no hurry, with a mentor sitting next to you; then you realise that dealing with traffic, giving the correct signals, obeying traffic lights and understanding all the controls is not so easy and can even be intimidating; then confidence grows as you gain the skills, but it still needs concentration; and finally you are driving with little conscious effort and able to think about route planning, finding a filling station, or where to go for lunch, while the driving is just a background task.

Stages of Change

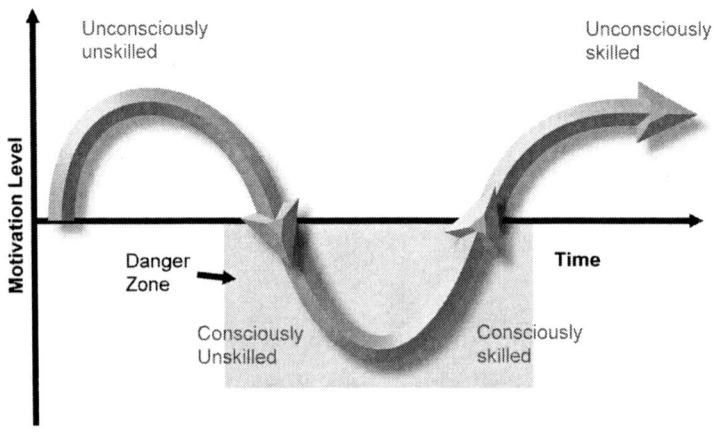

Figure 9: Stages of Change

The role of the change agent is critical in getting the organisation through the danger zone. It's not only the sales team who will get demoralised: the managers will see either little improvement or even a slump in sales as the sales people battle to apply the new skills. And while they are learning how to build relationships they will not be chasing down the quick wins, so the change agent needs both to encourage the sales team and manage the expectations of management.

Making it happen brings rich rewards. With the right strategy and the right tools, you don't have to wait until the end of the month to know what the results will be.

A Typical Timeline

Details of an implementation plan will always vary according to specific companies' needs, but what follows is a typical timeline that will give you a starting point for your own planning.

Pre-planning	Strategy sessions with management to determine the strategic customer focus and company alignment (Chapter 3: *Company Alignment*).
Day 1	Launch to sales and management teams. Explain in detail the principles and methodologies, and the strategy to be implemented. Schedule workshops to develop focus factors for different market segments and geographical areas.
Week 1-2	Focus factor workshops, involving various groups in addition to the sales and management teams.
	Group sessions with the sales team and first-line management to determine contact frequency targets.
Week 4	Deadline for first-line managers and sales team to have qualified all the customers and prospects in the database (Gold/Silver/Bronze), qualify individual contacts according to their influence levels, and to have gathered initial information, both personal and business, about the Gold and Silver decision-makers in their client companies.
	Senior managers should have a list of all Gold customers and make sure all resource departments are aware of who they are.
Week 5	Switch from talk to walk! By week 5 the sales team should start to implement CQM and management should be starting to measure them by CQM-oriented metrics.
	Senior managers should update the resource departments on the strategy implementation and

run workshops on how they can be proactive in delivering special service to Gold customers. Ideally, intermediate levels of special care should be devised for Silver customers as well.

First 4 months National sales manager must closely monitor the implementation process using first-line managers as lieutenants to drive the process. They should receive daily report-backs (at worst, twice-weekly). This high frequency reporting needs to be sustained for this initial period to get the new concepts and ways of working bedded down and turned into habits.

Maintenance Reporting and monitoring at senior sales management level can be dropped down to once or twice per month.

Regular meetings – again, once or twice a month – should be held with the sales people to handle objections and find ways around problems. Change produces discomfort and engenders resistance which must be countered with assistance and coaching.

Resistance to CQM

Introducing CQM into an organisation means change and carries with it a sense of risk. Some of that risk is real, most of it is imagined, but change always generates an element of fear, and with it comes resistance and objections. The objections are much the same in any organisation:

We don't have time to implement it. Of course not: you are so busy with unproductive sales calls and unprofitable customers that you barely have time to breathe. The fact is that implementing CQM does require an act of faith in the early weeks: you have to stop doing what has kept you going, however marginally or at whatever cost in time and effort, and start doing something different that will pay off in two or three or six months. Without commitment and support from management, you cannot do it. On the other side, if you don't change how you approach your customers, you will remain stuck on the treadmill you are on now.

There will be too many problems getting the different support departments to buy in. It's only too common for sales and the support functions (administration, logistics, manufacturing, accounts) to have an adversarial relationship. Most support divisions in one organisation or another have been scathingly referred to as the Sales Prevention Department. CQM is not a strategy for the sales team: it's a strategy for the entire organisation, and it has to be approached and sold as such. Alignment, discussed in *Company Alignment* (p. 21) is one of the three pillars of CQM.

But we will lose our small customers! There are two answers to this, either or both of which could apply: (1) not necessarily, and (2) so what? **Not necessarily** applies when you are over-servicing your small customers. The small customer who gets treated like a king by you and like dirt by your competitors will remain a customer if treated decently – but not royally – by you. A competent, efficient, courteous call centre can handle many more customers at lower cost than dedicated sales people. **So what?** applies where your small customers are costing you money. It's not unusual for small customers to be losing you money directly, i.e. where the total cost to the company of servicing them is higher than the profit made from them, or indirectly by costing you potential profit because the resources spent on them could be delivering far higher returns if applied elsewhere.

This is not new. We/XYZ Company tried this years ago. The basic principles of CQM strike some people as a flash of the blindingly obvious, or something they think they've seen before. Tried it, didn't work! CQM is a strategy that cannot work if it is only half-implemented, but that is what can easily happen. A champion in the sales division picks it up and runs with it, but without management buy-in from the top down and without enlisting the rest of the organisation. Then indeed the sales prevention departments get in on the act. Gold customers have their accounts frozen because they have purchased too much, or their deliveries are queued behind dozens of tiny, loss-making orders, or their shipments are mis-picked and they get the wrong quantities and sizes, and so it goes on. Then all the relationship-building that the sales team have done is destroyed, and "CQM doesn't work!"

It's too difficult to track. Tracking the quality of sales calls and customer relationships is harder and requires more thought than counting sales calls. Throw some money at a CRM package and the (meaningless) reports of numbers of calls will be churned out endlessly. They will give you the illusion of control, but seldom much more. Small wonder that the business and IT press frequently feature articles bemoaning the poor returns on CRM software investments.

Small customers today may be big customers tomorrow and we don't want to alienate them. There are two answers to this one:

1) How many of them will become bigger? You can't hang on to every small customer "just in case". Most of them never will, and part of your strategy has to be to provide a way of handling the small customers politely but efficiently. Telesales is one solution; another could be creating a second tier where the small customers are served by a sub-distributor, master reseller or wholesaler, as appropriate for your market.

2) If you are doing your homework properly you should be able to identify the customers with potential for growth. Remember that a Gold customer could be a small customer today, but has potential to become a big customer.

We don't know where or how to get information about our customers. Start off by identifying the kinds of information you need (a sample questionnaire can be downloaded from www.tracercqm.com/cqm.) To gather the information, tap resources such as secretaries and colleagues. Use central registers of company directors to get information like date of birth. Try searching on Google and Yahoo. Look in online who's who listings. Don't forget to gather negative interests as well: if your customer hates golf, don't invite her to a golf day; if he is Muslim, don't give him a bottle of Scotch at Christmas. Read the business press for profiles on your customer and prospect companies.

I can't call that often! I'll just irritate the customer! What can I talk about? These questions mean you don't know your customer well enough yet. Do your research, gather the information, and then look for ways to add value to each contact. If you are adding value, you will always be welcome.

Chapter Summary – Putting it into Practice

Buy-in from senior and first-line management is a key success factor in implementing CQM.

A successful implementation flows from a four-pillar business plan:

1. Identify the right clients

2. Develop strategies for Gold, Silver, Bronze; Attract, Expand, Sustain.

3. Set contact schedule targets

4. Identify ways to add value

Explain the four-pillar business plan to all involved.

Underlying requirements for the sales team are:

- Know the customer

- Have, and be encouraged to exercise, discretion over a budget

- Stick to the plan once you have developed it!

Involve as many people as you can to develop the strategy details.

Sales management must measure the key performance areas of the implementation. Their commitment, investment, and coaching abilities are the most critical factors in making it work.

Be prepared for a period of disillusionment and demoralisation (the danger zone), and have a champion or change agent to see you through it.

Expect to meet Resistance to Change, and prepare to counter it.

Bringing It All Together

This chapter pulls together the key elements that make for an effective implementation of a CQM strategy:

- Strategic skills development

- Getting the relationship between management and the sales team right

- Alignment and utilisation of company resources

- Buy-in

Strategic Skills Development

The standard approach to getting more out of the sales team is some combination of getting them to work harder and teaching them soft skills (salesmanship). Both have their place, of course, but the point that is generally missed is that these are not the areas where your biggest returns are usually to be found. If you are angling where there are very few fish, then no matter how hard you work or how skilfully you fish, you're not going to pull in much of a catch. You need to fish where the fish are, and in the context of developing a sales strategy that means identifying your customers (present and prospective) with the biggest potential. That, of course, is a central concept of this book.

Your sales team are your force in the field that needs to be gathering information to identify and quantify Gold customers, then targeting them and closing the business. They need to be given the strategic skills to understand what qualifies a customer or prospect as Gold or Silver, and to apportion their time appropriately.

Sales and Management Roles

In a nutshell: sales people do, first-line management coaches, senior management supports.

First-line sales management are the key to a successful implementation of CQM. They must understand and take ownership of the principles so they can coach their sales team, and are pivotal in getting both the sales team and senior management to buy in to the strategy. We discuss the roles of the different groups (sales, first-line management, senior management and support departments) in more detail later in this chapter when we look at how to get buy-in across the company.

Alignment and company resources

Aligning your business resources, business objectives and the market opportunity was the subject of Chapter 3 (*The Three Pillars of Business Strategy*, p. 21). These three components all interact with one another, and if they are not aligned then they work against each other.

Buy-in

No strategy, no matter how brilliant, will work without buy-in from the key players, and it will work best when you have buy-in across the board. Buy-in means getting commitment and active support from people, and in general is something you have to work to achieve. No matter how logical and clear the strategy may seem to you, it almost always has to be sold to the participants. Small amounts of negativity or even sabotage will have a disproportionate effect so widespread buy-in is very important.

The rest of this chapter discusses how to get buy-in.

Getting Buy-In

There's many a world-weary employee who's seen management coming back from a strategy meeting carrying the tablets of stone. After a day or two or three, the management team have come up with the Answer, distilled into a few punchy slides or slogans, and are ready to announce it proudly to the assembled peoples.

It doesn't work: if it has taken you days of thought and discussion following years of experience and observation to determine your strategy you can't expect to communicate it clearly in one announcement or even an hour or two's presentation.

Getting buy-in is a slow process: you need to convince people and get them to take ownership of the ideas, and you need to ensure that buy-in is widespread. It's not enough for the sales team to be fired up with the principles of CQM if accounts, logistics, technical support, receptionists, and management don't support them. We said in the previous chapter that there can hardly be a business of any significant size that has not had the phrase "Sales Prevention Department" used, usually about accounts but it can be applied to any of the others. While indeed there are some sales a business does want to prevent (because they will not be profitable), if your training and buy-in is done correctly you will not need a department to prevent them.

Buy-in Levels

Different groups in the business fill different roles in the sales process. Understanding those roles leads to understanding the level of buy-in needed.

Sales people are responsible for *Implementation*. The senior and influential ones are key: as they succeed others will follow. Involve them in the initial brainstorming that leads up to your strategy definition, for it must be the sales people, supported by coaching from line managers and clear communication of strategic objectives, who take final decisions on where customers and prospects fit in the Gold/Silver/Bronze model.

First-line managers will deliver *Empowerment*. They must own the strategy and drive it. They have to understand it so that they can coach the sales team, not just tell them what to do. They need to be monitoring the process and looking deeper than the raw numbers, collecting the right information to see that the right customers are getting the right amount and kind of attention.

Support departments require *Alignment.* They must be committed to supporting sales in accordance with the Gold/Silver/Bronze model, and understand the flow from Prospect through Attract and Expand to Sustain. There has to be a shared terminology so everyone understands and shares the common objectives.

Senior management's role is in *Alignment and Support.* They must also share the terminology, respect the sales team's customer assessments, and support the process in words and actions. For many senior managers, it will require an act of faith for the initial period, as they must stop chasing the numbers and focus instead on building the relationships *with the right customers.*

First-line and senior management are make-or-break to the implementation of CQM.

Involvement is vital, especially for first-line managers. Lack of understanding and commitment at this level will doom the process. Absolutely *all* first-line managers must be involved as it is they who will implement. Senior management support is equally critical: without it, the perception will quickly propagate that this is just another talk shop, a fad that will soon pass.

It is of course true that sales and support staff must buy in, and sales people are at the sharp end, but those who do not fit in can generally be replaced. It is much harder to rip and replace the management team.

Consistency Is Key

All levels from senior management to the sales team must be taught the same material, though the style and emphasis may vary. The typical cause of failure is to deliver different material to different levels: strategic consultancy for top management; management training for managers; soft skills for sales people. You end up with different groups having different terminologies, different objectives, and differing understanding of how to achieve the ultimate goals.

This is not to say that there is never a need for strategic consultancy, management training, or basic sales skills, but these other forms of training should be supportive of the principles of CQM. You can think of it as a military campaign: the generals need to have a strategic view of the campaign and the officers must direct the troops who will carry out the strategy on the ground, but if there is no common understanding of the relative value of different targets, the troops could be racking up successes knocking out farmhouses by the dozen, when a strike against a factory or airport would have many times greater impact at less cost.

Driving culture change

Usually CQM implementation involves a change in the company culture, not just changes in operational procedures. A culture change needs:

- **A disciplined implementation** that follows the roles discussed above under the heading *Buy-in Levels.*

- **Celebrating successes**. Not all successes have to be big ones. In the early stages in particular celebrate small wins like a sales person establishing a special connection with a Gold customer, perhaps through a shared interest. Get the good news out, and see that the information is shared. When sales deals can be celebrated, make sure you highlight the steps on the way to the closing of the deal.

- **Measure and track the right metrics**. Typical metrics are:

    o How many appointments are made in advance? If most of them are unplanned, then the sales people are not thinking strategically and are not seeing the major business influencers. The important people are seldom available at no notice.

    o Frequency of contact with the right people, in the right companies, not just call rate. (See *The Numbers Game* on p. 67)

    o How well do you know your customers? How many data points (birthdays, anniversaries, hobbies, interests, personal or business goals) do you have per customer contact? If you don't have this information, how can you add value to the customer?

    o Is your customer database appropriately sized? Do you have the right proportions of Gold/Silver/Bronze? (See *Too much or not enough Gold* on p. 51). Do you have in your sights potential business totalling two to three times your target?

- **Empower your salespeople**. Give them a discretionary budget, and give them general guidelines, but leave them with the authority to spend that budget.

- **Get your salespeople out of the office**. If you let your salespeople come into the office first thing to do their admin, you run the risk that they never get out, or they only get out late in the day. They should build their day around seeing customers first and coming into the office to do their admin at the end of the day. Free them of all unnecessary admin. Trust them, but measure them too (as in *Measure and track the right metrics* above).

- **Understand the problems of feedback and timing**. Feedback delayed is ineffective which is why diseases with long development times like AIDS spread so easily and why glacially slow criminal justice has limited deterrent value. We are not very good at linking cause and effect when they are months or years apart. A key role of the Sales Manager is to manage the long feedback cycles (see *Smoothing out the roller-coaster* on p. 73). If sales are down and the Sales Manager doesn't know why, it's a sign of trouble. What is less well understood is that if sales are *up* and the Sales Manager doesn't know why, it's just as ominous a sign of trouble! Sales are the outcome of structured selling activity: in a well-implemented CQM environment you know what sales are coming down the pipeline.

Chapter Summary – Bringing It All Together

Focus on developing the strategic skills of your sales people and first-line managers.

Your first-line sales management's investment into this process and their coaching abilities are the most critical elements for a successful CQM implementation. Work to get buy in from them, but also at all other levels and departments.

Accept that culture change is a slow process. Help it along with lots of feedback and celebration of early (and usually small) successes. Measure the right things: your sales team will react to how they are measured and rewarded, not to theoretical goals, and understand the need to compensate for the time lags between the right activities and the results coming through.

Keeping It Alive

It takes effort to change a company's culture, and it takes effort to sustain the change. Indeed, it takes effort to keep any company from slipping into mediocrity, to keep the focus sharp and enthusiasm up. Implementing CQM is no different: no matter how successful it is, if you don't spend time and effort on revitalising your team you will slip into bad habits. New hires also need to be inducted and cleansed of the bad habits they will have brought from their previous employers: most companies experience staff turnover of 10% to 20% per annum, so you have to ensure you keep the strategy fresh and true.

In this chapter we look at four tactics for keeping the CQM strategy alive: incentive schemes, creative targeting, involving the support personnel, and training. The points are illustrated with many case histories, as this is an area where no arguments are as powerful as demonstrated success.

Incentive Schemes

There are two simple rules for incentive schemes:

- Keep it simple.
- Target the results you want.

Keep it simple

An incentive scheme crafted around complex spreadsheets and multi-factored formulas may appeal to the accountants and some managers, but it won't work for the rank and file. If the connection between achievement and reward is too convoluted, the sales person or sales support person will not be clear in his or her mind what has to be done to win the reward. If you can't readily see how your actions and achievements get you closer to your goal, you will not be focused on the right actions. Worse, you may unwittingly work against yourself and only realise too late that you have done so, leaving you totally demoralised.

Overly complex incentive schemes also breed mistrust. The complications can be seen as a way of cheating the staff out of their rewards, a perception that is sometimes wholly justified. It's only too common to come across management who are against sales people earning more than they do, even if it means that the company is doing very well out of it. Complicated schemes often amount to little more than ensuring no-one does *too* well out of them, and your sales team will figure that out long before they understand the detailed mechanisms.

Target the result you want

When you dangle a carrot, be very careful where you put it, because that is where your sales team will go. If you base an incentive on turnover growth, you will get turnover growth; if you target new customers, that's what you will get; if call rate is your criterion, you will get high call rates. All of these (except the last) can be good and appropriate targets, depending on the needs of your business, but usually they are not; usually you are looking for growth in profitability, and increasing turnover, number of customers and call rate can all actively hurt profitability rather than boosting it.

Incentivising on turnover (when turnover growth is not really the goal) is probably the commonest mistake companies make, typically because they are not willing to let the sales people know what margins are being made. When you do this, your sales people will get the business at any price, using every scrap of discretion you give them to offer the maximum discount. From the sales person's perspective, a 10% discount does not make much difference to their progress towards a turnover target, and if it secures the deal (in their mind), it's worth the price. From the company's perspective, a 10% discount could be costing the lion's share of the profit, or even, in a very competitive market, pushing the deal into a loss.

Case study

Plant Hire, an equipment rental company, incentivised the sales team on turnover, and first-line managers were continually fielding requests for "specials" to close the deal. As a result, they had an enormous number of contracts with very thin margins, and the smaller ones were actually costing them money once the administrative overhead was taken into account. Some deals were going through as low as 2% below prime.

The sales targets were changed to a basic turnover requirement, whereafter profitability was taken into account. The results were immediate and dramatic. Requests for special rates stopped, and the non-stop reports of competitors offering lower rates dried up. Deals started being signed at far higher rates, sometimes as much as 18% *above* prime. The number of deals dropped, but profitability rocketed.

Case study

Stationery Co, a supplier of stationery and filing systems dealing directly with companies, operated with no published price list, just an internal reference price. Stationery Co was struggling to grow its business: turnover was edging up, but the bottom line was not improving.

A review of their customer base and the value being

derived from different customers highlighted the problem: the sales team were measured and rewarded on sales volume. The sales incentive was re-modelled around margins. Over the next 10 months, profitability doubled.

In both case histories above, the problem the companies had was that the sales team wanted to drop prices to get business more easily. They had almost no incentive to want to sell at a higher price. When the incentive schemes were changed, they had good reason to want to achieve a higher price: adding a few percent to the deal made a big difference to their reward. They now had good reason to want to sell to customer based on value, not on price.

Creative Targeting

A good incentive incorporates an element of showmanship, and should also not be based on a target that seems so far out of reach that it will just engender a "why bother" response.

Dry figures don't put sparkle into people; it needs something to make the goal tangible and exciting.

Case study

A new sales manager in a computer rental company committed to double the book in 12 months, a target generally considered too ambitious, and meeting considerable resistance from the sales team. At the start of the financial year, the new target was launched with a display and demonstration of the latest, top-of-the-range PDA (Personal Digital Assistant) in a range of colours, and the sales team were promised one each in their choice of colour once the team made target.

At the time, the PDAs were a very hot "must-have" accessory, and they added a tangible, emotional fillip to the normal sales commissions which could be referenced throughout the year. With the prize clearly in mind, the sales team set about planning how they would achieve the growth.

They made target.

Case study

In another case, the sales manager wanted to grow sales by 25%, but instead of presenting it to his team as a humdrum "achieve 25% growth", he changed it to "achieve 25% growth, but do it in 10 months, not 12". This changed the challenge from "how do we do more of the same?" to "what must we do faster and differently?" with the little bit of a cushion gained by building in two months spare at the end. In the event, they achieved target, in ten months, and went on to exceed target in the next two.

Case study

A pharmaceuticals company split their sales team into a new products group and an established products group, and brought in a new manager to run the established products group. Unspoken, but generally understood, was that the supposedly best sales people were in the new products group.

The new manager was expected to achieve moderate growth but primarily to keep the routine, cash cow business going, but he determined to do better, so he got his sales team together and gave them a challenge: to show the company that they were actually the best team, and to do it by making target before the July conference (nearly six months early). The sceptics outside the team said it couldn't be done, as to make the goal they would have to wrest huge market share from the generic drugs.

The 'B' team achieved their goal. They grew turnover in their product set by 45%, pushing their market share from 60% to almost 95%. In July, at the company sales conference, they flaunted team T-shirts and had uncontested bragging rights.

This targeting worked so well because it was audacious, but without negatives. It was a case of "let's see if we can over-achieve by making target 6 months early". Not making that ambitious target was not going to mean a failure to meet the annual target: there was plenty of time in hand for that. But aiming for the much more ambitious target was exciting, necessitated some re-thinking of how to go about building sales, and made achieving the underlying target easy.

Sales Support Personnel

It's not enough to pay lip service to the contribution that sales support personnel make to sales: they should also have a direct interest in sales targets being achieved.

Where appropriate, it's best to have support people and sales people working as teams, rather than having a general pool of support staff serving all the sales staff. The more direct the link between closing specific deals and personal incentives, the more effective the incentives are. It also greatly simplifies prioritisation of customers when support staff are not torn between a pushy sales person's Silver customer and a less-pushy rep's Gold customer. It's generally not realistic to expect a sales person to defer allocation of resources to another sales person for the greater good of the company: after all, you employ sales people who are driven to achieve personal goals!

Case study

A distributor of PCs and laptops had downsized from 160 employees to 35, but set a goal of growing their sales by 50% in the next calendar year. To focus everyone in the company on their goal, management promised to pay every employee, from the cleaning staff upwards, a bonus of R20000 (about $3000) if the company reached the target, not by the end of December, but by the end of September.

The effect was electrifying. Every single employee was

focused on the goal and eager to do whatever they could to win "their" R20000. Everyone had to plan to work faster and smarter, and the support team, from support engineers to secretaries, cleaners and the tea lady, formed a flying wedge behind the sales people, encouraging them and egging them on.

In the event, the company missed the deadline by one week. The Managing Director awarded the company a bonus of R10000 for getting so close, and they went on to close the year at 83% growth over the previous year.

Training

Training for new sales people should be run as often as needed but not less than twice a year, lest new sales people be given too much time to settle into bad habits or contaminate existing staff. A typical course would take three days, and the usual pattern is: day one, explain the principles and it sounds good; day two: overcome objections; day three, start to teach the skills. It can be hard to eradicate old conceptions of how selling should be done. In one company, a senior manager had to be brought in to confirm to the trainees that the CQM approach that they were being taught was indeed how the company operated.

Management also need regular re-training to keep the principles clear in their minds and affirm how CQM is working for them. Management is always under pressure to produce short-term results, and the temptation to bend the rules and focus on sales instead of the process "just for this month/quarter/year-end" is ever-present. It's worse when they succumb and get a short-term fillip, which reinforces the behaviour, and before you know it you are back in the boom and bust cycle (see *Smoothing out the roller-coaster* on p. 73), not knowing where your next quarter's business is coming from.

Chapter Summary – Keeping It Alive

The way you set incentives determines what you will get. Make very sure that your incentives are aligned with your business objectives.

Creative incentives add excitement and can make seemingly impossible targets still worth aiming for – and sometimes achieving!

Involve your support personnel in the sales effort, make them part of the team, and structure incentives that include them.

Keep the culture alive by training all new sales people and line management entering the company on the principles and practical implementation of CQM.

11

In Conclusion

The two principles underlying Customer Quality Management (CQM) are well-known and much talked about: the 80/20 rule, and that business is about relationships.

The 80/20 rule states that generally the majority of the results come from a minority of the causes. In the sales context, it says that roughly 80% of your results (turnover, profit, market share) will come from roughly 20% of your base. The peculiarity of businesses is that although this is widely recognised as a truth, it is seldom used to guide the allocation of effort and resources, and even when it is, businesses are rarely clear on how to use that information.

There are other places where you will find the 80/20 split, usually working against you:

- 80% of your sales effort is typically being spent on customers who represent only 20% of the potential

- 80% of your time is spent on internal issues, 20% on your customers

- 80% of your logistics effort is going into 20% of the value of the shipments.

Identifying these areas is a rich source of finding scope for efficiencies.

The second principle is that business is about relationships, which has the further qualification that it is about relationships with people who are whole people: they have lives and interests outside of their business. Relationships need to be built around both business and personal issues.

CQM puts both of these principles into a new framework, where the emphasis is on *quality*: the quality of your customers, and the quality of your relationships with them. Sales management traditionally has put far too much focus on *quantity*: the number of customers and the number of interactions (typically, sales calls). This focus on the wrong metrics is often compounded by Customer Relationship Management (CRM) software which fails to measure the important things and just reports on numbers. An inappropriate CRM system imposes its rules on your sales strategy whether you like it or not: you get what you measure, and what is measured is determined by the designers of the software, not by you.

CQM is about managing the quality of your customers and the quality of your sales calls or customer contacts. Focussing the right attention on the right customers will maximise the returns you get for your sales effort. Often, the right customers are invisible to you because you are so busy dealing with the wrong ones. The biggest mistake made in sales is to rate customers based on the business they are giving you instead of on the business they could be giving you. Existing large customers can blind you to small customers with enormous potential that you have not developed, and can prevent you from realising that your biggest customers are very likely ones you are not dealing with yet.

Devoting resources to customers in proportion to the business you are actually getting from them is at best a retention strategy. The opportunity for massive growth lies in attracting and developing potential.

There are steps that must be taken on the way to implementing a good CQM strategy.

- You have to have clear in your mind what constitutes a good customer for your business. To do this, you need to ensure that you have alignment of the three pillars of a successful strategy: business resources (what you have), market opportunity (what the market wants), and business objectives (what you want to achieve), which we discussed in Chapter 3, *The Three Pillars of Business Strategy*.

- You have to have a methodology for categorising your customers and prospects so you know which of them are truly the most important to your business. (Chapter 4 – *Focus Factors*)

- Develop a customer contact plan and devise ways to build relationships with the key influencers in your key customers, whilst finding ways of dealing with low-value customers that will not sap limited sales and support resources, even going so far as to divest yourself of them. (Chapter 5, *Building Relationships in a CQM Environment*, and Chapter 6, *Combining Frequency and Value-Add*).

- Gather information about your customers. You cannot add value to their lives if you don't know what is important to them. (Chapter 7, *Know Your Customer*)

One of the biggest hurdles to a successful implementation of CQM is shifting the management focus from the output (sales) to the input (the sales process). Putting pressure on the sales figures leads to the classic sales roller-coaster: sales people are praised and rewarded when the orders come in, and being human, they tend to relax their sales effort. When the sales drop off and they start scrambling to generate new business, they are being punished.

If the process is right, and the principles of CQM are being applied, the sales will follow.

Here are some comments from companies that successfully implemented CQM:

"Four-fold increase in sales within 6 months!"
> *Wayne Brunyee, Sales Director,*
> *Information Technology Industry*

"150 – 200 % sales growth within 5 months in our 4 most under-performing cells!"
> *Marieta Frampton, National Sales Manager, Banking Industry*

"85 % increase in sales year-on-year!"
> *David Drummond, Managing Director, IT Hardware Company*

"I am already excited to see the results!"
> *Johan Louw, Managing Director, Pharmaceutical Industry*
> *(they achieved 73 % profit growth after tax in the*
> *first year)*

Index

10/80/10 principle, **113**

3 pillars of business strategy, **21**

4 pillar business plan, **101**

80/20 principle, **2**, 14, 26, 39, 41, 113, 139

Activity consistency, **70**, 73, 76

Alignment, 21, **31**, 33, 37, 123, 124, 126

Business influencers, **62**, **83**

Business objectives, 22, **26**, 27, 28, 40

Business resources, 22, **30**, 40

Business/personal mix, 83

Buy-in, getting, **125**

Call frequency. *See* Contact frequency

Call Quality Management, **17**, 18, 78

Case study
A good recovery, 107
A home run, 108
Building a relationship, 71
Business equipment finance, 17
Chemotherapy product, 78
Creative Incentive, 136
Creative targeting, 135

Creative Targeting, 134
Derailed implementation, 106
Equipment rental, 133
Good and bad implementations, 106
Logistics company, 99
MedicSupply - pharmaceutical, 52
MediTrak - health care, 36
Office equipment rental, 58
Office filing systems, 15
Office stationery supplier, 16
Pharmaceutical company, 25
Stationery and filing systems, 133

Change agent, **114**, 116

Change, stages of, **115**

Coaching, 104, **112**, 126

Commitment model, **77**

Contact frequency, **67**, 74, 77, 105, 110, 128

Creative targetingt, **134**

Customer Quality Management, 7, **13**

Customer Relationship Management (CRM), 5, 8, **18**, 19, 20, 69, 99, 106, 111, 120, 140

Customerculture, **23**

Dot com crash, 5

First-line management, 9, 88, 104, 109, 112, 117, 124, 126

Focus factors, 37, **43**, 44, 47, 48

Gold – too few or too many, 51

Incentive schemes, 111, **131**, 134

Information gathering, 63, 72, 77, 84, **93**, 96, 112, **121**

Lottery tickets, 67

Magic, 4

Market opportunity, 22, **28**, 40

Measurement and reporting, 111

Multi-level selling, 61

Performance metrics, 6

Personal/business mix, 83

Pipeline, building, **105**

Proactive targeting, **70**

Relationships, 2, 3, 37, 41, 53, 65, 75, 76, 79, 80, 104, 108, 126, 139, 140, 141

Reporting and Measurement, 111

Resistance to CQM, **118**

Sales activity cycle, **73**

Sales support personnel, **136**

Senior management, 43, 88, 103, 107, 108, 109, 117, 126

Stages of change, **115**

Submarine commander's dilemma, 91

Support resources, 30, 89, 103, 109, 126, 136

Targeting, **134**

Timeline, typical, **116**

Tracer CQM, 38, 111

Training, **137**

Value-add examples, 82, 95

Further Information

Scientia Performance Consulting coaches businesses in the principles and implementation of Customer Quality Management.

The term Customer Quality Management was coined by the authors in the course of looking for a concise term that would encapsulate the principles that had proven so effective in re-energising businesses. A related company, TracerCQM, has developed a CQM application that goes beyond CRM, embodying the concepts in *The Invisible Customer*, and providing both sales people and their managers with the tools they need to plan, capture, manage and report on their CQM strategy.

Material referenced in this book (the CQM implementation plan template, the customer information-gathering questionnaire, and other related information) can be found at **www.tracercqm.com**.

The authors can be contacted as follows:

Cobus van Graan
Email: cobus@tracercqm.com
Mobile: +27 83 628 3084

Dr Chris Crozier
Email: chriscrozier@telkomsa.net
Mobile: +27 83 377 7289

Cobus van Graan, B.Juris., LLB (UPE)

Tap into the practical experience of someone who has dramatically enhanced the sales performance of SME's and large corporate companies. Cobus specialises in the implementation of sales strategies and more specifically the implementation of key account strategies. He has been involved in sales, sales management and key account management since 1990. Cobus has an excellent track record in different industries and has an uncanny way of turning theory into practice, and practice into results.

Dr Chris Crozier, B.Sc. (Wits), Ph.D. (Cantab)

Chris is an engineer by training, with a Ph.D. in advanced communication theory from Cambridge University, UK. He has worked for companies big and small, with most of his career having been spent in entrepreneurial start-ups. He is currently a director and part-owner of a software company as well as being an author and presenter.

ISBN 142512250-7

9 781425 122508